BLEEDING THE PATIENT

THE CONSEQUENCES OF CORPORATE HEALTHCARE

David Himmelstein, M.D. and
Steffie Woolhandler, M.D., M.P.H.
with Ida Hellander, M.D.

D0062010

Common Courage Press

Monroe, ME
Philadelphia, PA

Library of Congress Cataloguing-in-Publication Data

Himmelstein, David U.
Bleeding the patient: the consequences of corporate healthcare /
David Himmelstein and Steffie Woolhandler ; with Ida Hellander.
p.cm.
Includes bibliographical references.
ISBN 1-56751-206-2 (cloth) -- ISBN 1-56751-207-0 (pbk.)
1. Health maintenance organizations--United States. 2. Managed
care plans (Medical care)--United States. 3. Medical policy--United
States. 4. Insurance, Health--United States. I. Woolhandler, Steffie.
II. Hellander, Ida. III. Title.

RA413.H54 2001
362.1'0973--dc21   2001017274

Common Courage Press
P.O. Box 702
Monroe, Maine 04951
207-525-0900; fax: 207-525-3068
orders-info@commoncouragepress.com

www.commoncouragepress.com

First Printing

Contents

The Failure of "Free Market" Healthcare

Once, health policy wonks preached the gospel of market competition and managed-care, promising efficient, consumer-responsive care. Today, market fundamentalism is less credible. After two decades of market-driven health policy, costs are again soaring, coverage is contracting, and health maintenance organizations (HMOs) have joined tobacco firms in the basement of public esteem. Yesterday's true believers have lapsed into cynicism. *The New York Times*, an early booster of market medicine, now warns that there may be no solution to healthcare's woes.

Reality has swamped zealots' arguments for market solutions. Nihilism is their new defense. "Things are bad. But there is no alternative (TINA)." TINA claims come in two flavors: (1) Extending coverage, bridling HMOs' power, or improving quality would break the bank. And: (2) Although high quality national health insurance is affordable and theoretically feasible, it is politically impossible, the opposition is too rich, and our democracy too weak.

This book confronts the first of these arguments directly. Many of healthcare's worsening woes emanate from market medicine and its greed-is-good business ethic. A widening circle of patients and caregivers suffer to enable a narrow band of investors and executives to profit.

Non-profit national health insurance can expand coverage, improve care, and limit costs by slashing healthcare bureaucracy and outrageous profits. Our resources for care—hospitals, clinics, high-tech machinery—are already plentiful, our personnel ready and willing, and our current spending levels are sufficient. The experience of many nations—that spend less and get more healthcare—proves that national health insurance works.

Rebutting the second argument—that our democracy is too weak—requires direct political action. We hope to contribute to that by arming activists and organizers. The book's charts were developed as speaking aids, and are available in slide form and as graphics files via the Internet (WWW.PNHP.ORG). For each chart we have added commentary placing the data in context, and providing supplementary information. In addition, a précis at the start of each chapter integrates the fragments of data into a coherent argument. Pieced together, these chapter précis form a narrative outline for speakers preparing a slide presentation.

This book arises from the work of the 9000 members of Physicians for a National Health Program (WWW.PNHP.ORG). Numerous colleagues have pointed us to useful data, given feedback on previous versions of these graphics, and helped shape our ideas. Drs. Gordy Schiff, Deb Richter, and Quentin Young played major roles in the book's development. The support and friendship of Dr. David Bor, and other colleagues at Cambridge Hospital/Harvard Medical School, has been essential to this project. Financial support from The Open Society Institute made this book possible.

CHAPTER 1

Rich Country, Poor Care

Forty-three million Americans lack health insurance today, as many as were uninsured when Medicare and Medicaid were passed in the mid-1960s (graphic 1). Despite the economic boom of the 1990s the number of uninsured increased by 8 million between 1990 and 1999 (2). Millions more will lose coverage if the economy flattens. Contrary to popular myth that the uninsured are mostly the hard-core unemployed, three-quarters of those without coverage are children or working adults (3). Though most Americans with private insurance have coverage through an employer, no inherent logic links coverage to employment (4); other developed nations provide health coverage as a right of citizenship. Even many full-time workers in the U.S., especially minority workers, lack insurance (5). Despite promises that former welfare recipients could continue their Medicaid coverage when the Clinton administration slashed welfare rolls in the mid-1990s, several million poor women and children lost coverage. (6).

For those with insurance, the situation is also getting worse. Workers are paying a higher share of premiums (and larger co-payments and deductibles) as firms shift costs onto employees (7). Seniors have also faced rising out-of-pocket costs. By accelerating cost increases for Medicare recipients, proposals to introduce market-based reforms in Medicare (e.g., vouchers or premiums support programs) would make the situation worse (8). While the uninsured face the gravest problems, few Americans have adequate coverage. Most who need long-term nursing home care face a grim financial prospect: they pay out-of-pocket until the payments impoverish them, making them

7

eligible for Medicaid. Indeed, private insurance covers only 7% of nursing home costs (9). The financial consequences of needing healthcare affect a broad cross section of Americans: nearly half of all bankruptcies involve illness or medical debts (10).

Choices over healthcare have also been narrowed with the increasing intrusion of market forces in medicine. One example: 42% of privately insured adults were offered only one health plan (11). The responsiveness of corporations to consumer demands is illusory. Patients rarely switch health plans voluntarily; three quarters of those changing plans are forced to do so by their employer or because they have changed jobs (12).

Lack of coverage, insurance hassles, and other problems paying for care endanger the health of millions. Many, fearing financial ruin from medical bills, forego care for potentially life-threatening symptoms such as chest pain or a breast lump (13). Even in emergencies, HMOs often erect barriers to care (14). Financial suffering often compounds the burden of illness, especially for terminally-ill patients and their families (15). Women frequently delay prenatal care because they're uninsured or unable to pay (16). Many of the uninsured lack other necessities of life, forcing them to choose between medical care, food, rent, or utilities (17).

1. The Crisis is Widespread

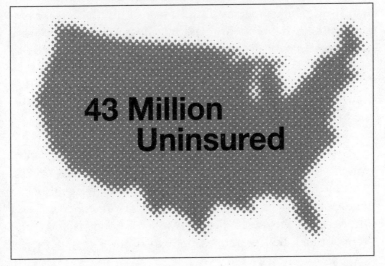

43 Million Uninsured

Those who lack coverage suffer most dramatically. Currently, about 43 million Americans are uninsured. But this figure understates the extent of the crisis. While 43 million are uninsured at any one time during the year, about 55 million people lack coverage for at least one month. Over the course of 28 months about 67 million are uninsured for at least one month. Hence, about one quarter of the population has experienced a recent bout of "uninsurance."

The situation is particularly bad for young people. About 10 million (13.9%) children under 18 are uninsured at any one time. Among young adults age 18–24, 28.9% are uninsured. During 1995–1996, 23.1 million of the total of 70.8 million children in the U.S. went without health insurance for at least one month.

Poorer families have the highest uninsurance rates, but even the well-to-do are at risk. 24.1% of persons in households with annual incomes below $25,000 were uninsured in 1999, vs. 8.3% of those with household incomes greater than $75,000.

People with serious illnesses or disabilities depend predominantly on public programs. While 46% of health costs for persons without disability are paid by private insurance, private insurance accounts for only 27% of spending for those with disabilities; 18% is paid out-of-pocket, 30% by Medicare, 10% by Medicaid, 10% by other public programs, and 4% by other sources. More than half of all HIV-positive Americans are covered by public insurance policies, while private insurance covers only 19%; 29% are uninsured.

Uninsurance rates are highest in the South and West. Among the states New Mexico had the highest rate, 25.8%. Arizona, California, Louisiana, Nevada, and Texas also had uninsurance rates of 20% or higher. Connecticut, Iowa, Minnesota, Missouri, Pennsylvania, Rhode Island, and Vermont had the lowest rates, 6.9% to 10%.

2. A Strong Economy is Not a Cure

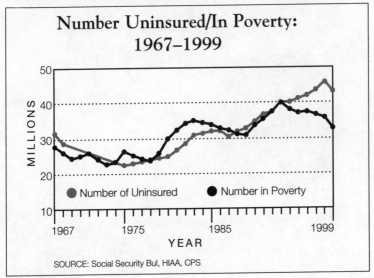

Number Uninsured/In Poverty: 1967–1999

SOURCE: Social Security Bul, HIAA, CPS

Improvements in the economy won't solve the crisis of uninsurance. Over the past 22 years the number of uninsured Americans has increased by about 20 million. This rise paralleled an increase in poverty rates until 1993. But while the recent economic expansion has decreased poverty, it has left large numbers of uninsured.

Private health insurance steadily declined between 1980 and 1993; the proportion of the population under 65 with private coverage fell from 79.5% to 70.2%. Since 1993, private coverage has risen little, despite the booming economy. Meanwhile, Medicaid coverage has fallen: 3.9 million fewer people were covered by Medicaid in 1999 than in 1993.

Between 1993 and 1999 the proportion of children who were uninsured increased from 13.7% to 13.9%; the number of uninsured children rose by 855,000.

3. Only Politicians are Safe

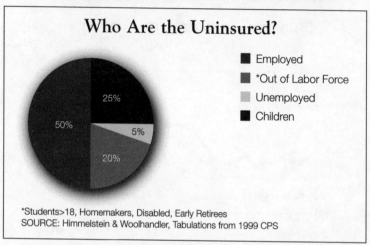

Who Are the Uninsured?

- ■ Employed
- ■ *Out of Labor Force
- ■ Unemployed
- ■ Children

25%

50%

5%

20%

*Students>18, Homemakers, Disabled, Early Retirees
SOURCE: Himmelstein & Woolhandler, Tabulations from 1999 CPS

While the poor and members of minority groups are least likely to have health insurance, substantial numbers of people from all walks of life lack coverage. Non-Hispanic whites make up the largest number of uninsured, 21.4 million in 1999, though they have the lowest proportion uninsured of any ethnic group (11%). Hispanics account for 10.9 million of the uninsured and African-Americans for 7.5 million. 13 million of the uninsured had family incomes above $50,000 per year, while an additional 14 million had family incomes between $25,000 and $50,000 annually.

Uninsurance rates are particularly high (greater than 30% in 1998) for workers in agriculture, construction, and household services. 20% or more of workers employed in retail establishments, repair services, personal services, entertainment, and the forestry and fishing industries are uninsured. While there are no uninsured legislators, about 5% of physicians and nurses are uninsured, as are 7% of teachers and university professors, and more than 10% of clergy. Indeed, 12.2% of all healthcare workers, 1.36 million people, are uninsured, and 1.2 million uninsured children live in a household with a healthcare worker, accounting for 10.1% of all uninsured children. Among the poor, workers are less likely to be insured than non-workers.

4. Do the Uninsured Just Need Jobs?

5. Full-time Jobs Provide Little Protection

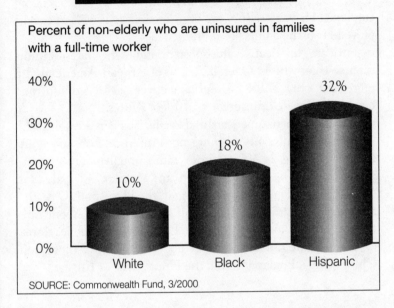

Percent of non-elderly who are uninsured in families with a full-time worker

SOURCE: Commonwealth Fund, 3/2000

Contrary to a popular perception that those lacking insurance are mostly unemployed, about two-thirds of the uninsured are employed workers and their families. 19 million full-time workers (16.4% of full-time workers) are uninsured, as are 5.2 million part-time workers (22.4% of part-time workers). 16.5% of men and boys are uninsured; 14.6% of women and girls.

Hispanics are more than twice as likely as non-Hispanic whites to lack health insurance. 33.4% of all Hispanic-origin Americans are uninsured, including 32% of full-time workers. 36% of Hispanic males are uninsured, as are 31% of females. Strikingly, 44% of all poor Hispanics have no insurance. Elderly Hispanics are more often uninsured than seniors from other ethnic groups; 5.2% of Hispanics age 65 and over lack coverage (as compared to 0.9% of all seniors).

Fewer than half of all Hispanics, 47%, have private insurance, compared to 74% of non-Hispanic whites. Among employed Hispanics, 36% are uninsured. About 60% of unemployed Hispanic adults are uninsured.

African-Americans suffer substantially higher rates of uninsurance than whites. Overall, 21.2% of African-Americans are uninsured; only 55.8% have private coverage. 18% of full-time black workers are uninsured, vs. 10% of whites.

21.1% of Asian-Americans and Pacific Islanders are uninsured.

Among immigrants who are not citizens, 42.6% are uninsured, including 24.4% of those with annual family incomes above $60,000. Of those born in Mexico, El Salvador, Guatemala, or Haiti who are living in the U.S. (both U.S. citizens and non-citizens), about half are uninsured. About one-third of U.S. residents born in the Dominican Republic, Korea, or Vietnam are uninsured, as are about one-fifth of those from China, Cuba, England, India, the Philippines, or Russia.

6. Off the Rolls and Off the Insurance

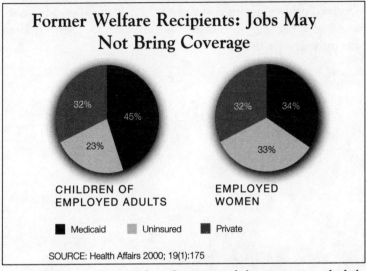

Former Welfare Recipients: Jobs May Not Bring Coverage

CHILDREN OF EMPLOYED ADULTS: 32%, 45%, 23%

EMPLOYED WOMEN: 32%, 34%, 33%

■ Medicaid ▨ Uninsured ▨ Private

SOURCE: Health Affairs 2000; 19(1):175

Healthcare coverage has deteriorated for women and children who have moved off welfare, despite politicians' promises to the contrary. The federal legislation that "reformed" welfare supposedly protected those leaving welfare from losing their Medicaid coverage by mandating that states continue Medicaid for former recipients. But most states have not complied with the law, and the federal government has failed to enforce it. As a result, Medicaid enrollment has dropped sharply, and the number of uninsured has risen.

Medicaid enrollment stabilized in 1999 after a decline of 1.1 million in 1998, and a fall of 2.5 million in 1997. Hence, the uninsurance rate for poor children under 6 climbed from 20.1% in 1997 to 23.6% in 1998. Women have also lost ground recently; while the number of uninsured females fell by 785,000 in 1999, this did not even make up for the increases of 947,000 in 1998, and 931,000 in 1997. Since 1992, the number of uninsured females has increased from 17 million to 20.5 million (from 13.1% to 14.6% of all women).

Among women leaving welfare who found jobs, only 32% obtained private health coverage; 34% continued on Medicaid, while 33% became uninsured. The situation for their children was only slightly better.

7. Insured Workers Shoulder a Bigger Burden

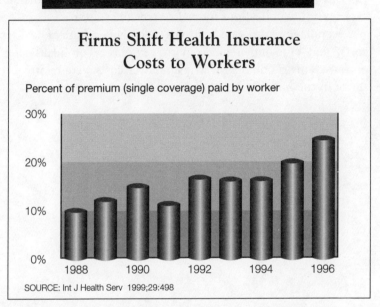

Firms Shift Health Insurance Costs to Workers

Percent of premium (single coverage) paid by worker

SOURCE: Int J Health Serv 1999;29:498

In recent years employers have shifted costs onto employees and limited employees' choice of plans. Between 1988 and 1996, the proportion of the premium (for individual coverage) paid by employees in small firms rose from 12% to 33%. In large firms the employee's contribution to the premium was 13% in 1988 and 22% in 1996. As a result, employee costs for individual coverage in small firms rose from $12.00 per month in 1988 to $56.00 per month in 1996, an increase of 21% per year. For family coverage the increase was even larger, averaging 23% per year; rising from $34.00 in 1988 to $175.00 in 1996. Meanwhile, total premiums increased only 8% per year, indicating that employees shouldered a greater and greater portion of the cost.

Retirees are also being squeezed by former employers seeking to curb healthcare costs. For retirees aged 65 and older, the proportion of large firms offering health benefits fell from 80% in 1991 to 71% in 1997. The number of employers placing dollar caps on future obligations for retiree coverage also rose sharply.

Overall, employees are bearing a much larger share of health costs, and enjoying a much narrower choice of healthcare options. This is one reason why employer costs were relatively stable in the mid-1990s.

8. The Future Could Be Worse

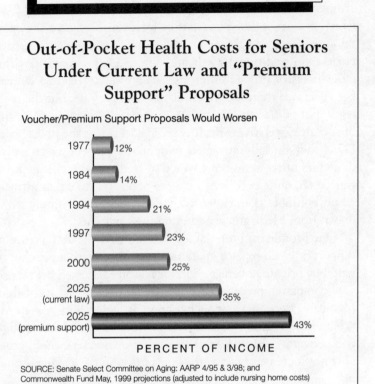

Out-of-Pocket Health Costs for Seniors Under Current Law and "Premium Support" Proposals

Voucher/Premium Support Proposals Would Worsen

- 1977: 12%
- 1984: 14%
- 1994: 21%
- 1997: 23%
- 2000: 25%
- 2025 (current law): 35%
- 2025 (premium support): 43%

PERCENT OF INCOME

SOURCE: Senate Select Committee on Aging: AARP 4/95 & 3/98; and Commonwealth Fund May, 1999 projections (adjusted to include nursing home costs)

Medicare covers virtually all seniors. Yet seniors, like the other segments of the population, are spending an increasing share of their incomes for medical services. By 2000, the average senior was spending 25% of total income for medical care. Medicare currently covers a little less than half of all medical expenses of the elderly, about the same proportion that was covered by insurance before Medicare was passed.

Medicare offers scant coverage for nursing homes or prescription drugs, and requires seniors to pay steep co-payments and deductibles for hospital and physician care. These gaps in

Medicare coverage have driven many seniors into Medicare HMOs, private insurance plans that subcontract with the government-funded Medicare program. Initially these HMOs, which receive a fixed capitation fee from Medicare for each senior who signs up, offered enrollees more comprehensive coverage than traditional Medicare. The plans promised that the efficiencies of private enterprise would allow them to deliver better service than the government could provide. But the reality is quite different. Many Medicare HMOs made easy profits by recruiting relatively healthy seniors who cost the plans little. Plans that initially attracted patients by offering coverage of drugs and other items not covered by traditional Medicare have started charging enrollees large premiums. HMOs that attracted unprofitable (i.e., expensively ill) seniors have simply withdrawn from Medicare, abandoning their patients.

One prominent proposal for reforming Medicare ("premium support") would replace guaranteed coverage with a voucher to help buy private coverage. But, for reasons discussed below, private companies provide less coverage for each dollar spent than Medicare. Because the voucher amount would fully cover only a bare-bones policy, poorer seniors wouldn't be able to afford good coverage. Moreover, the size of the vouchers would probably not increase as fast as the cost of insurance, leaving seniors paying more.

9. Chronic Care, a Financial Nightmare

Who Pays for Nursing Home Care?

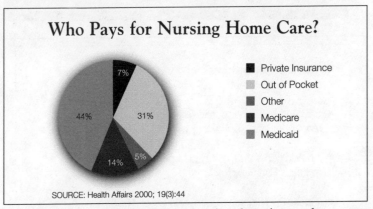

Legend:
- Private Insurance
- Out of Pocket
- Other
- Medicare
- Medicaid

SOURCE: Health Affairs 2000; 19(3):44

At present patients and their families directly pay about one-third of nursing home costs. Medicaid and Medicare pay for most of the rest. Private insurance plays a minor role, covering only 7% of long-term care costs.

Public insurance and out-of-pocket payments also cover most home care costs. Moreover, more than 70% of those receiving long-term care (3.2 million people) rely exclusively on informal (unpaid) caregivers. About 22% use both formal and informal care, while 5% use only formal care.

Of the more than 7 million informal caregivers:

- 75% are women,
- 35% are themselves over 65 years old,
- 34% are in poor health,
- 10% have given up paid employment to assume the care of their loved one,
- and 8 of 10 spend at least 4 hours every day providing care.

Such personal devotion can never be replaced by the assistance of even the kindest of strangers. Rather than being supplanted by formal care, it must be valued and supported.

10. Illness and Medical Costs: A Major Cause of Bankruptcy

- 45.6% of all bankruptcies involve a medical reason or large medical debt

- 326,441 families identified illness/injury as the main reason for bankruptcy in 1999

- An additional 269,757 had large medical debts at time of bankruptcy

- 7 per 1000 single women, and 5 per 1000 men suffered medical-related bankruptcy in 1999

SOURCE: Norton's Bankruptcy Advisor, May, 2000

Medical problems and bills are responsible for nearly half of all personal bankruptcies. As the authors of the study cited above note: "The bankruptcy courts are populated not only with the uninsured, but also with those whose insurance does not cover all the financial consequences of their medical problems." 79% of the families filing for bankruptcy had at least some health insurance. Insurance is supposed to provide a safety net against catastrophe. Yet those who identified a medical problem as a cause of their bankruptcy were as likely to have health insurance as people who filed for bankruptcy but reported no medical problem.

These data on actual bankruptcy filings confirm previous indirect estimates of the risk of heavy out-of-pocket medical costs run by privately-insured Americans. In 1977, 12.6% of privately insured people under age 65 had a 1% risk of a catastrophic illness that would cost them more than 10% of family income. By 1994, 18.5% of people were underinsured using this same definition. The underinsured included 23.1% of blacks and Hispanics, and 17.7% of whites; 17% of males and 20% of females; 16.7% of those who rated their health as excellent and 34.7% of those describing their health as poor. As mentioned elsewhere, adding those who are underinsured to those who are uninsured for all or part of the year, about one-third of Americans are uninsured or underinsured.

11. Many With Insurance Lack Choice

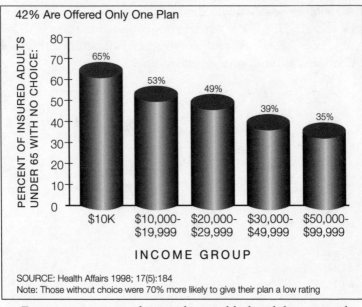

42% Are Offered Only One Plan

PERCENT OF INSURED ADULTS UNDER 65 WITH NO CHOICE:

- $10K: 65%
- $10,000-$19,999: 53%
- $20,000-$29,999: 49%
- $30,000-$49,999: 39%
- $50,000-$99,999: 35%

INCOME GROUP

SOURCE: Health Affairs 1998; 17(5):184
Note: Those without choice were 70% more likely to give their plan a low rating

Forty-two percent of insured non-elderly adults report that they have no choice of health plan. Those without a choice are far less satisfied with their health plan, and less likely to trust their doctor, especially if enrolled in managed-care. According to another national survey by the consulting firm KPMG Peat Marwick, 80% of employees in small firms are offered only a single health plan, and an additional 15% are offered only two plans. In the smallest firms, those with fewer than 10 employees, 91% are offered only a single health plan option. Among large firms, 47% offer only a single health plan choice, and an additional 24% offer a choice among only two plans.

These data belie the claim that private insurance and market-driven care are offering patients choices.

12. Disrupting Continuity of Care

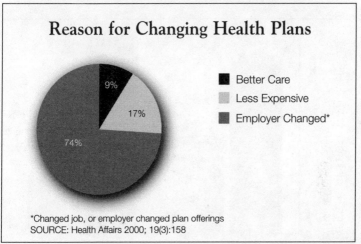

Reason for Changing Health Plans

- Better Care
- Less Expensive
- Employer Changed*

9%
17%
74%

*Changed job, or employer changed plan offerings
SOURCE: Health Affairs 2000; 19(3):158

About 17% of privately insured Americans change plans each year, often disrupting the continuity of their care. Those switching insurance are twice as likely as others to change their usual source of care. Only 9% switched plans to get better care. Three-quarters were forced to switch because they changed jobs or because their employer changed plan offerings. An additional 17% switched in search of a cheaper plan. Thus, choice remains a prerogative of employers, not patients, assuring that quality plays little role in driving plan selection.

According to data from another survey, among those forced to change plans in the past 5 years, 50% were offered only a single option for new coverage.

13. The Uninsured Forego Care for Serious Symptoms (Sx)

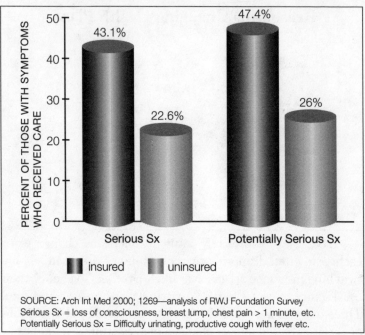

SOURCE: Arch Int Med 2000; 1269—analysis of RWJ Foundation Survey
Serious Sx = loss of consciousness, breast lump, chest pain > 1 minute, etc.
Potentially Serious Sx = Difficulty urinating, productive cough with fever etc.

Patients who are uninsured face barriers in getting care, and receive lower quality care. The study shown above is only one of the dozens finding that uninsurance is a health hazard. An analysis in the *Journal of the American Medical Association* concluded that death rates for the uninsured are about 25% higher than for comparable people with insurance; thousands die each year from lack of coverage.

The uninsured also experience high rates of malpractice. In a large study of adverse events and medical negligence suffered by inpatients at New York hospitals, 40.3% of the adverse events suffered by uninsured patients were due to negligence, compared to 29.1% for Medicaid patients and 20.3% for those with private insurance. African-Americans also suffered a higher rate of negligent adverse events, 36% vs. 23.6% for whites and others. The poor were also at higher risk, 36.5% of adverse events being due to negligence vs. 25% among the non-poor. In a multivariate analysis, being uninsured was associated with a 2.35 fold increase in the proportion of adverse events due to negligence. Most of this excess among the uninsured and Medicaid patients occurred in emergency departments or in the labor and delivery suite.

In a 1997 telephone survey of 43,771 people, twice as many reported that their access to needed care had deteriorated since 1994 as indicated that their access had improved. Low income families and Hispanics were more likely to report worsening access. Only the elderly, virtually all of whom are covered by Medicare, were unlikely to experience declining access.

14. HMOs Give New Meaning to the Term "Emergency"

Patients Refused Authorization for ER Care

- 8% to 12% of HMO patients presenting to two ERs were denied authorization

- Authorization delayed care by 20 to 150 minutes

- Of those denied:
  - 47% had unstable vital signs or other high risk indicators
  - 40% of children were not seen in f/u by primary MD
  - Eventual diagnoses included: meningococcemia (2), ruptured ectopic (2), shock due to hemorrhage (2), septic hip, PE, MI (2), ruptured AAA, pancreatitis, peritonsillar abscess, small bowel obstruction, unstable angina, pneumothorax, appendicitis, meningitis (3).

SOURCE: J Emerg Med 1997; 15:605; Acad Emerg Med 1997; 4:1129; Ann Emerg Med 1990; 19:59

Many insurers now require a gatekeeper to authorize care, even in emergencies. For primary care physicians, such requirements often mean annoying administrative paperwork and phone calls. For emergency departments (EDs), the administrative headache can be substantial, and lead to payment denials even in clearly emergent cases. For patients, the consequences are often graver. At the very least, prior authorization delays care while the ED contacts the primary care doctor. In some cases, such as those shown above, unstable patients are denied care; children's problems are never evaluated; and care is delayed in urgent, life-threatening situations.

The image that Americans, especially the uninsured, abuse the ED is not borne out by data. Uninsured Americans use no more ED care than the insured, though the uninsured use less of most other types of care. Hence, the ED is a vital source of care for the uninsured—and particularly for black men—and for others with limited access to primary care.

Nor is it true that high cost ED care is responsible for much of the expense of our system. Americans use less emergency care, per capita, than Canadians, whose healthcare system is less costly. Though the charges for an ED visit in the U.S. are high, cutting down on ED visits saves little money unless EDs are shut down. Most ED costs are "fixed." If an ED is open and staffed, seeing a patient for an earache adds very little to the real costs of running the department.

15. Financial Suffering at the End of Life

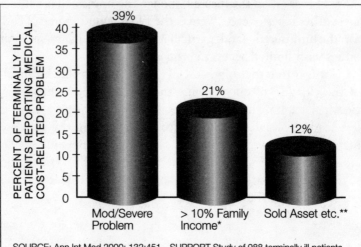

SOURCE: Ann Int Med 2000; 132:451—SUPPORT Study of 988 terminally ill patients
* Out-of-pocket medical costs > 10% of household income
** Patient or family sold assets, took out mortgage, used savings or took extra job

Financial concerns amplify the suffering of the dying. In a large study of the terminally ill, 39% of the patients or their families reported that the costs of illness were a moderate or severe problem. Medical costs consumed more than 10% of family income in 21% of cases, and 12% of families experienced severe financial distress—being forced to take out a mortgage, seek an extra job, sell assets, or use up their savings.

Terminally ill patients with problematic medical costs were also more likely to feel that they were a burden for their families.

As debate rages over terminally ill patients' right to choose how they die, one point is rarely discussed: Patients too often face a Faustian choice between extending their lives on the one hand, or saving their family money on the other.

16. Why Women Delay Prenatal Care When They Know that They are Pregnant

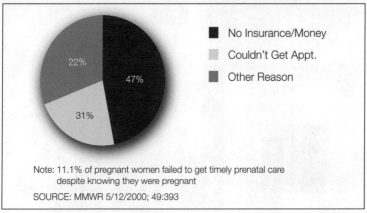

No Insurance/Money

Couldn't Get Appt.

Other Reason

Note: 11.1% of pregnant women failed to get timely prenatal care despite knowing they were pregnant

SOURCE: MMWR 5/12/2000; 49:393

The U.S. has the lowest prenatal care rate of any developed nation. 17.5% of pregnant women, and 27.7% of pregnant black women, fail to receive prenatal care during the first trimester. No other wealthy nation has a rate worse than 10%. Fully 7.3% of pregnant black women fail to receive <u>any</u> prenatal care before the third trimester. Inadequate prenatal care contributes to the high U.S. infant mortality rate.

The major reason women who know they are pregnant delay prenatal care is lack of insurance or money. In addition, insurance problems may underlie the difficulties getting an appointment that 31% of women cited as causing their delay. Many physicians refuse or limit care to Medicaid patients because of low fees.

17. Food, Rent, Utilities, or Health Insurance?

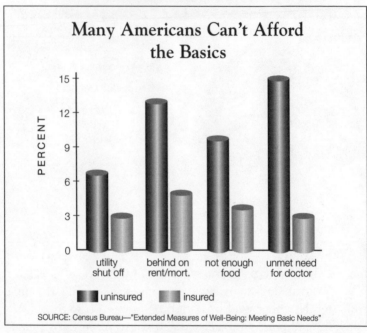

Many Americans Can't Afford the Basics

SOURCE: Census Bureau—"Extended Measures of Well-Being: Meeting Basic Needs"

A Census Bureau survey found deprivation surprisingly common in the U.S., despite the recent economic boom. The data on Americans who forego the basics also belie claims that medically uninsured adults choose to spend money on less important things. Large numbers of the uninsured are unable to afford housing, utilities, and food. 6.6% (vs. 2.9% of the insured) had a utility shut off in the past year; 13.1% (vs. 4.9%) had fallen behind on their rent or mortgage, and 9.7% (vs. 3.4%) had been unable to afford enough food. Not surprisingly, 14.9% of the uninsured (vs. 3.1% of those with coverage) reported an unmet need to see a doctor.

CHAPTER 2

Increasing Inequality

THE RICH GET RICHER, THE POOR GET SICK

Why must people living in the wealthiest nation on Earth struggle to get the care they need—and often lose the battle? Glaring inequalities in health and healthcare mirror a broader economic and social polarization in the U.S. The share of wealth held by the wealthiest 10% of Americans grew from 49% to 69% in the past two decades (18). While the average per capita income is higher in the U.S. than in Canada, this statistic hides an important skew: all of the U.S. advantage accrues to the wealthy. Most Americans have less disposable income than their Canadian counterparts (19). The U.S. has the highest poverty rate among affluent, developed nations (20). Meanwhile, Americans work longer hours than workers in any other nation—even longer than in Japan (21). Rising inequality, persistence of extreme poverty, and mandatory sentencing laws that substitute jail for drug treatment are packing our prisons (22).

Racial inequalities in infant death rates, which shrunk in the late 1960s in the wake of civil rights successes, have expanded to historic new highs (23). And overall death rates among African-Americans remain far higher than among whites, mostly due to an excess of preventable diseases (24). When minorities get sick, they may be unable to find adequate treatment even when they can afford it; 75% of pharmacies in minority neighborhoods in New York don't carry an adequate supply of narcotics for cancer pain relief (25). Increasing the number of minority physicians is vital to improving access to care for poor and minority patients (26). Yet, the rollback of affirmative action portends a shortage of minority physicians for decades to come (27).

18. The Rich Get Richer...

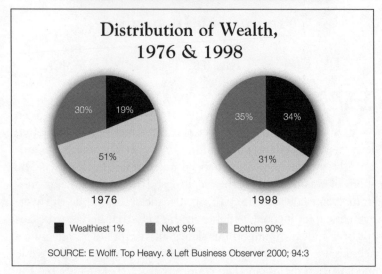

Distribution of Wealth, 1976 & 1998

1976

1998

■ Wealthiest 1%　■ Next 9%　■ Bottom 90%

SOURCE: E Wolff. Top Heavy. & Left Business Observer 2000; 94:3

In the post-World War II boom, Americans, rich and poor, saw rapid increases in their incomes. Between 1950 and 1978 the lowest-income 20% of the population saw a 138% increase, and the top 20% had income growth of 99%. However, since 1979 mainly the rich have gotten richer. Between 1979 and 1998 the richest 5% of families have increased their incomes by 72.8%, while the poorest 20% saw a 2.7% fall in income (corrected for inflation).

The polarization of wealth is even more extreme than the polarization of income. In 1976, the wealthiest 1% of Americans owned 19% of total assets. By 1998 they owned 34%. Meanwhile, the bottom 90% of Americans owned 51% of assets in 1976, falling to 31% by 1998. Bill Gates' personal fortune is equal to the total net assets of the poorest 40% of American families. The fruits of economic growth over the past 20 years have mostly accrued to the wealthiest 5% of Americans.

19. Money in Our Pockets: Comparisons with Other Countries

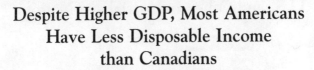

Despite Higher GDP, Most Americans Have Less Disposable Income than Canadians

% Difference In Income Between Canada and U.S., 1995
(minus indicates U.S. is lower)

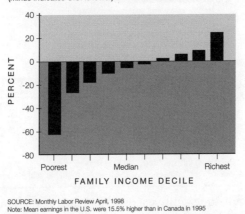

SOURCE: Monthly Labor Review April, 1998
Note: Mean earnings in the U.S. were 15.5% higher than in Canada in 1995

Overall, the U.S. is wealthier than Canada; average earnings are 15.5% higher. Yet income is so unequally distributed in the U.S. that 60% of Americans have less disposable income than their Canadian counterparts. For instance, the poorest 10% of Americans have incomes about 60% lower than the poorest 10% of Canadians.

Canada has modestly higher tax rates than the U.S., and uses those tax dollars to support national health insurance, more public universities, and better welfare and retirement systems. As a result, needed medical care is available to all, college and medical school tuitions are low, and few Canadians live in abject poverty.

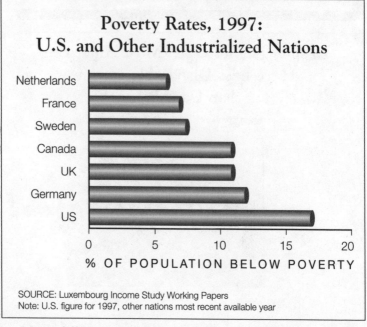

Poverty Rates, 1997:
U.S. and Other Industrialized Nations

% OF POPULATION BELOW POVERTY

SOURCE: Luxembourg Income Study Working Papers
Note: U.S. figure for 1997, other nations most recent available year

Many full-time, full-year workers earn less than a poverty level income. 19% (18 million people) of full-time workers do not earn enough to bring a family of four above the poverty line. In 1998, this included 14.1% of all male full-time, full-year workers, and 23.7% of females.

The social programs implemented during the 1960s in the U.S. cut poverty rates almost in half to 23 million. Unfortunately, most of the progress made during the 1960s was erased between 1973 and 1993, when the number below poverty peaked at 39.7 million. Over the past six years, the number below poverty has fallen only modestly, to 32.3 million in 1999. Even with this improvement, 16.9% of all children are still living in poverty.

More Americans live in poverty than in other affluent nations. U.S. poverty rates are 60% higher than Canada's or the U.K.'s, twice as high as Sweden's, and almost three times those of the Netherlands. Since the average income in the U.S. is similar or higher than in these other nations, our high poverty rate is due to income inequalities.

21. Are Our Social Ills the Result of Laziness?

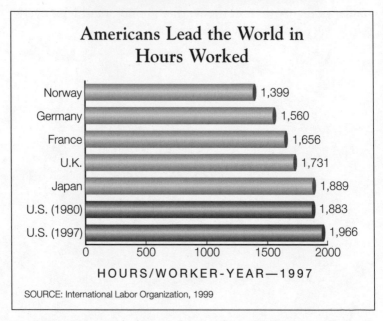

Americans Lead the World in Hours Worked

Country	Hours
Norway	1,399
Germany	1,560
France	1,656
U.K.	1,731
Japan	1,889
U.S. (1980)	1,883
U.S. (1997)	1,966

HOURS/WORKER-YEAR—1997

SOURCE: International Labor Organization, 1999

Americans work longer hours than Japanese or German workers, and our increasing wealth has brought a longer work week and less leisure time. Moreover, as more women have entered the workforce, the total number of hours worked per family has skyrocketed.

U.S. workers also get far less vacation time than workers in other nations. American workers average 10.8 paid vacation days per year, vs. 24 in Japan, 24.5 in the U.K., and 29.9 in Germany.

22. America's Fastest Growing Social Program

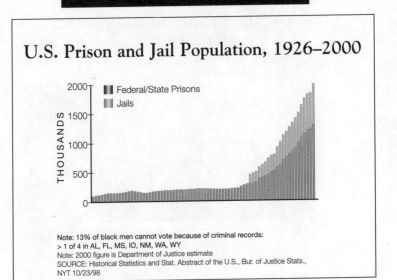

U.S. Prison and Jail Population, 1926–2000

Note: 13% of black men cannot vote because of criminal records:
> 1 of 4 in AL, FL, MS, IO, NM, WA, WY
Note: 2000 figure is Department of Justice estimate
SOURCE: Historical Statistics and Stat. Abstract of the U.S., Bur. of Justice Stats.,
NYT 10/23/98

From the early part of this century, until the mid-1970s, the number of Americans in prison remained relatively stable. However, since 1975 the prison and jail population has exploded. The U.S. now has the second highest incarceration rate of any nation (after Russia). Indeed, a larger proportion of African-Americans are now imprisoned in the U.S. than the proportion of blacks who were in imprisoned in South Africa under Apartheid. The State of California spends more for prisons than for the public university system.

This explosion of incarceration takes place in a highly unequal society that neglects education, healthcare, and other social needs. Mandatory sentencing laws for drug offenses are filling prisons, reflecting the policy that substance abuse should be treated as a criminal rather than as a medical issue.

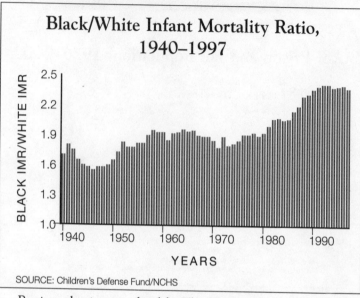

Black/White Infant Mortality Ratio, 1940–1997

Y-axis: BLACK IMR/WHITE IMR (2.5, 2.2, 1.9, 1.6, 1.3, 1.0)

X-axis: YEARS (1940, 1950, 1960, 1970, 1980, 1990)

SOURCE: Children's Defense Fund/NCHS

Racism also impacts health. The black/white infant mortality gap has widened over the past 20 years. This gap narrowed during World War II, coincident with integration and improved opportunities for African-Americans. The ratio rose again during the 1950s and early 60s. It fell sharply in the late 60s and early 1970s, during the implementation of landmark civil rights legislation, affirmative action, and new social programs in response to the civil rights movement. With the retrenchment of the late 70s, and the 1980s and 1990s, the racial gap has once again widened.

24. The Mortal Consequences of Racial Inequality

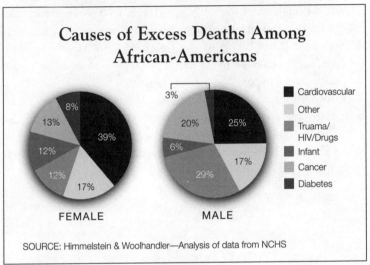

Causes of Excess Deaths Among African-Americans

FEMALE: 39%, 17%, 12%, 12%, 13%, 8%

MALE: 3%, 25%, 17%, 29%, 6%, 20%

Legend: Cardiovascular, Other, Truama/ HIV/Drugs, Infant, Cancer, Diabetes

SOURCE: Himmelstein & Woolhandler—Analysis of data from NCHS

Many of the excess deaths among African-Americans (relative to whites) are due to conditions that are amenable to medical care. Roughly one-third of the excess is due to cardiovascular disease, much of that preventable by the detection and reduction of high blood pressure and cholesterol. Many of the excess cancer deaths are also due to inadequate detection or substandard treatment. Similarly, good care for pregnancy or diabetes can prevent many deaths, but is unavailable to many African-Americans.

Health inequalities are not solely due to health insurance issues. African-American seniors, virtually all covered by Medicare, are 17% more likely to die than white seniors, and suffer 14% more hospitalizations. Black seniors undergo elevated rates of leg amputations and other undesirable medical procedures. In contrast, their rates of preventive and outpatient care are substantially lower. For instance, for every 1,000 Medicare beneficiaries of each race, there were 500 influenza immunizations among whites and 313 among blacks. Mammography rates were 33% lower among blacks than among whites. Though blacks were 74% as likely to have heart attacks and other manifestations of ischemic heart disease (blockages in arteries that bring blood to the heart muscle) as whites, they received only 46% as many angioplasties, and 40% as many coronary artery bypass surgeries as whites.

Poor seniors are also disadvantaged. For instance, immunization rates are 26% lower among poor whites than among the affluent. Income-related differences account for some, but not all, of the racial differences, suggesting that other forms of institutionalized racism are involved.

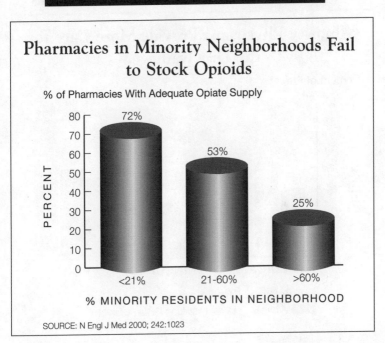

Pharmacies in Minority Neighborhoods Fail to Stock Opioids

% of Pharmacies With Adequate Opiate Supply

72%
53%
25%

PERCENT

<21%   21-60%   >60%

% MINORITY RESIDENTS IN NEIGHBORHOOD

SOURCE: N Engl J Med 2000; 242:1023

One form of institutionalized racism is segregation of minorities into neighborhoods where medical services and supplies are unavailable. In many neighborhoods, even those able to pay for medications may not be able to obtain pain relievers. In New York neighborhoods where more than 60% of residents are from minority groups, only 25% of pharmacies stock a minimally adequate range of narcotic pain relievers.

Studies have also shown that physicians are far less likely to provide adequate pain relief to minority cancer patients, or to minority patients with fractures.

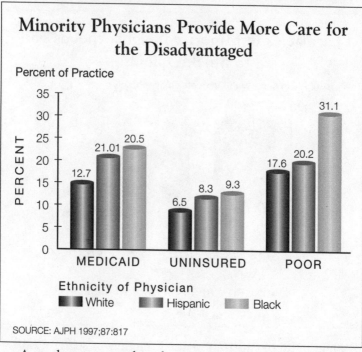

Minority Physicians Provide More Care for the Disadvantaged

Percent of Practice

Ethnicity of Physician
White   Hispanic   Black

SOURCE: AJPH 1997;87:817

An adequate supply of minority physicians is vital to improving access for minority and poor patients. While poor patients account for 17.6% of the practices of white physicians, they make up 31.1% of the patients in African-American physicians' practices, and 20.2% of the practices of Hispanic physicians. Similarly, uninsured patients account for 6.5% of those in white physicians' practices, 9.3% of patients in African-American physicians' practices, and 8.3% of those in Hispanic physicians practices. Medicaid patients account for 12.7% of patients of white physicians, 20.5% of black physicians' patients, and 21% of Hispanic physicians' patients.

African-American patients account for 14.2% of the patients in practices of primary care physicians of European-American origin, as compared to 48% of the patients in African-American physicians' practices. Hispanic patients comprise 7.6% of the practices of white physicians vs. 44.8% of the practices of Hispanic physicians. Asian patients comprise 3% of the practices of white physicians vs. 16.9% of the practices of Asian-American physicians.

27. But the Solution is Blocked

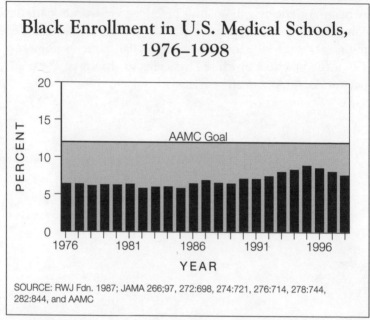

Black Enrollment in U.S. Medical Schools, 1976–1998

SOURCE: RWJ Fdn. 1987; JAMA 266;97, 272:698, 274:721, 276:714, 278:744, 282:844, and AAMC

Three decades ago the American Association of Medical Colleges established the goal of enrolling African-Americans in medical school at the same proportion as their representation in the population as a whole. Despite modest progress in the late 1960s and again in the early 1990s, the goal was never achieved. In the past 4 years progress has been reversed. The recent assault on affirmative action has discouraged many minority students from applying to medical school.

CHAPTER 3

The Inefficiencies of
Private Healthcare

RATIONING IN THE MIDST OF PLENTY

T he suffering of many who are ill-served by the U.S. healthcare system paradoxically coexists with a surplus of resources to take care of those in need. While millions of Americans are denied needed care, 300,000 hospital beds lie empty every day (28), and health policy leaders warn of an impending surplus of physicians (29). Meanwhile, a growing army of health bureaucrats fights to keep sick patients away from idle healthcare resources and personnel (30, 31).

28. Empty Hospital Beds

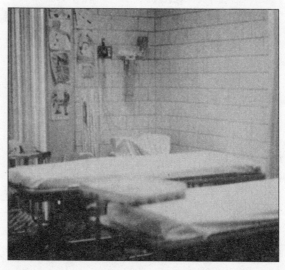

The U.S. currently has a substantial over supply of hospital beds and other hospital resources. One-third of all hospital beds (350,000) are empty on an average day in this nation, while millions are denied needed care. Moreover, MRI machines, operating rooms, and other expensive equipment often lie idle.

These idle facilities mean that hospitals could deliver additional care at low additional cost. Allowing a patient to recuperate for an additional day, or admitting an uninsured patient to a bed that would otherwise lie empty, costs relatively little. Due to the current over supply of hospital beds and high technology equipment, expanded care for the uninsured could be accommodated without building many new facilities.

29. Idle Medical Personnel

Many analysts foresee an impending surplus of medical personnel in the United States, and a few medical specialties are already overcrowded. Enough well-trained professionals are available to take care of the uninsured—if our healthcare was organized rationally.

30. The Art of Paper Pushing

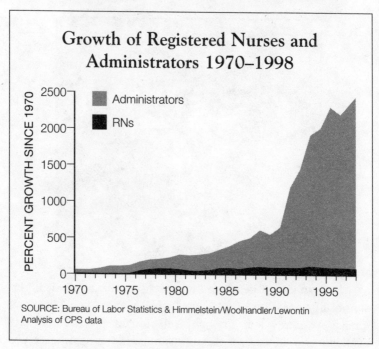

Growth of Registered Nurses and Administrators 1970–1998

PERCENT GROWTH SINCE 1970

- Administrators
- RNs

SOURCE: Bureau of Labor Statistics & Himmelstein/Woolhandler/Lewontin Analysis of CPS data

The number of registered nurses working in healthcare in the U.S. has grown steadily. However, this growth is dwarfed by the rapid increase in the number of administrators. Between 1970 and 1998, total healthcare employment in the U.S. grew 149%, while the number of managers in healthcare grew 2,348%. If the U.S. reduced its health administration work force to Canada's levels (on a per capita basis), we would employ 1.4 million fewer managers and clerks. Despite much lower medical spending in Canada, Canadians receive slightly more nursing and other clinical care than Americans.

31. Growth of Physicians and Administrators, 1970–1998

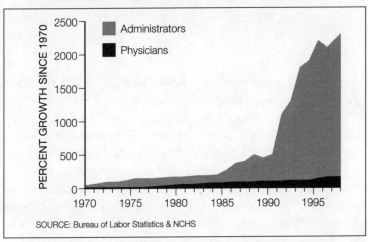

SOURCE: Bureau of Labor Statistics & NCHS

Administrators are the most rapidly growing segment of the healthcare labor force. Between 1970 and 1998 the number of health administrators increased more than 24 fold, while the number of physicians and other clinical personnel increased about 2 1/2 fold. It apparently takes substantial administrative effort to keep sick patients out of empty hospital beds and away from idle physicians.

Growth in administration results from a system focused on profit: a hospital must work diligently to squeeze payment from an insurance company. And each insurer must do the reverse: since every dollar paid out in claims means less profit. Here, the administrators are at war, wrestling over who gets to keep the healthcare dollar.

Similarly, HMO administrators strive to recruit healthy, profitable patients and to exclude the expensively ill who are unprofitable; and many thousands of bureaucrats minutely supervise the work of doctors and nurses, trying to shape care to increase profits.

CHAPTER 4

Profit-Driven Managed Care

THE DISEASE, NOT THE CURE

Recent health policies have encouraged market-based strategies—an expanded role for investor-owned firms, reliance on competition to control costs and streamline care, and the emergence of managed-care. While pro-market theorists like Alain Enthoven (a Defense Department official and war planner during the Vietnam War) often trumpet healthcare competition, only half of Americans live in regions with sufficient population density to support competition; a town's only hospital cannot compete with itself. Thus, even if competition were part of the solution, it would be irrelevant for half of Americans (32).

But competition in healthcare isn't part of the solution; it's part of the problem. An HMO that provided excellent care for the expensively ill would risk attracting too many of these unprofitable patients, and face financial disaster in a competitive market. Conversely, HMOs profit from healthy patients, and research shows that HMOs provide care for them on a par with fee-for-service medicine (fee-for-service is the traditional style of medical practice in which doctors receive a fee for each visit). But sick lower-income patients face a 21% higher risk of dying in HMOs than in fee-for-service (33), and elderly people with chronic conditions also fare poorly in HMOs (34). Sick HMO patients report substantial barriers to care (35). HMOs also impede access for Medicaid patients (36), and score poorly in consumer satisfaction surveys (37).

Several studies demonstrate that HMOs provide poor quality care to sick patients. Stroke patients covered by HMOs receive less specialist care than do patients in fee-for-service medicine (38), get less rehabilitation care, and more often end up in nursing homes (39). Medicare HMO patients needing home care receive fewer home visits and have worse outcomes than similar patients covered by the traditional Medicare program (40). HMOs in New York selectively refer heart surgery patients to the hospitals with the highest surgical death rates (41), presumably because those hospitals give the HMOs a price break.

HMOs often undertreat people with mental illnesses. Depression is less likely to be recognized, appropriately treated, or improved even in good HMOs than in fee-for-service settings (42). Many HMOs and employers subcontract mental health services to for-profit managed mental healthcare firms that routinely provide substandard care (43). Less than one-third of primary care physicians report that they can always or almost always obtain high-quality mental healthcare for their patients (44). And the share of total health benefits going to psychiatric care has fallen by nearly half during the past decade (45).

In areas where managed-care predominates, the corrosive effects of the focus on profit is clear: charity care shrinks (46) and research suffers (47). Academic leaders attest to the damage that managed-care has inflicted on research, teaching, care of the underserved, and collegial relations (48). Nurses report being forced to care for more and sicker patients, and to neglect the human side of care (49).

32. Where is Competition Conceivable?

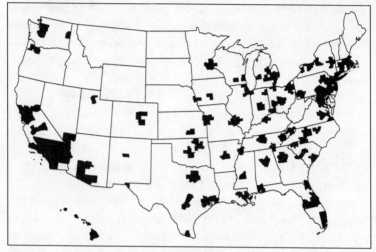

Figure 1. Health Markets with Populations ≥ 360,000 in the United States. Metropolitan areas (health markets) with populations ≥ 360,000 are shown in black.

Source: NEJM 1993; 328:148.

In smaller cities and in rural America, population is too sparse to support meaningful competition in healthcare. A town's only HMO or hospital cannot compete with itself. The minimum feasible size for a comprehensive HMO is about 400,000 enrollees. While it is unclear how many HMOs are needed to foster real competition, three competitors in the same area is probably a minimum. Even three HMOs that dominate a region may tacitly collude to drive up prices, enlarging the pie of healthcare dollars (and profits) rather than fighting for the biggest piece. In order to support three comprehensive HMOs a market area's population must exceed 1.2 million. Yet only 42% of the U.S. population lives in metropolitan areas of this size.

The majority of the 50 states (26) have no market area with this large a population.

Even with assumptions much more sympathetic to competitive market-based healthcare, competition does not appear to be feasible in much of our nation. On the map above, market areas with populations greater than 360,000 are shaded black. For the 36% of Americans who live in the unshaded areas, including 9 entire states, competition among healthcare providers is inconceivable.

To quote the noted economist John Kenneth Galbraith: "...the neoclassical monopoly or oligopoly exploits the power that goes with being one, or one of a few, sellers in the market. Such power allows for prices and profits that are higher and output that is smaller than would be the case were sellers more numerous. In consequence consumers pay more and have less product or service than is necessary or desirable...and the distribution of income is distorted in favor of the monopolist" (*Economics and the Public Purpose*, 1973).

33. WARNING: HMOs Can be Hazardous to Your Health

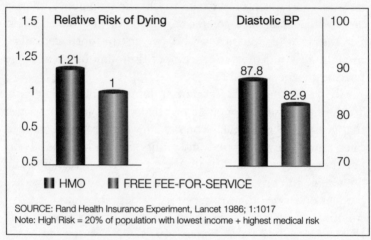

SOURCE: Rand Health Insurance Experiment, Lancet 1986; 1:1017
Note: High Risk = 20% of population with lowest income + highest medical risk

The only randomized control trial of health insurance arrangements was conducted by the Rand Corporation under a contract from the federal government starting in the 1970's. The study randomly assigned patients to a variety of fee-for-service health insurance plans, or to an HMO—Group Health Cooperative of Puget Sound, among the best HMOs in the United States. The researchers then followed the patients for three to five years, and determined their state of health at the end. For most patients, care at Group Health Cooperative was as good as in the fee-for-service sector. However, lower income patients (the poor were excluded from the study) who were in poor health at the start of the study fared badly in the HMO. Their risk of dying was 21% higher in HMO care than in the fee-for-service sector, largely due to a deterioration in their blood pressure control. If the same pattern holds nationwide, forcing all Americans into HMOs would cause an excess of about 100,000 deaths each year.

Yet despite this robust data showing that even good HMO's are harmful to the health of the vulnerable, both Democrats and Republicans have continued to push Americans—especially the poor and lower income workers—into managed-care plans. Moreover, most of these plans are far inferior to the plan studied in the Rand experiment.

34. The Elderly and Sick Poor Do Worse in HMOs

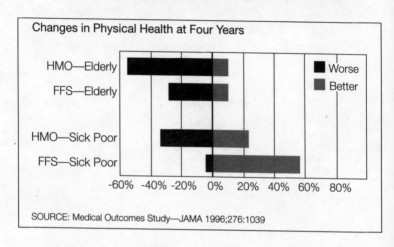

Changes in Physical Health at Four Years

SOURCE: Medical Outcomes Study—JAMA 1996;276:1039

The Medical Outcomes Study was a carefully designed observational study of elderly patients and poor patients with chronic conditions who were treated in HMOs or in fee-for-service settings. The HMOs were some of the best plans in the nation, including Harvard Community Health Plan and the Ross-Loos Clinic in California. During the four years of the study, the health of elderly patients in HMOs was more likely to deteriorate; the health of poor patients in HMOs was both more likely to deteriorate and less likely to improve than the health of patients in fee-for-service.

Moreover, in the course of this study many sick HMO patients switched into fee-for-service care, while few sick fee-for-service patients switched to HMO care. Hence, the study documented a pattern of sick people preferentially leaving HMOs. Since sick people cost money, this pattern of sick people exiting is highly profitable for HMOs.

35. Sick HMO Patients: Profits and Care Don't Mix

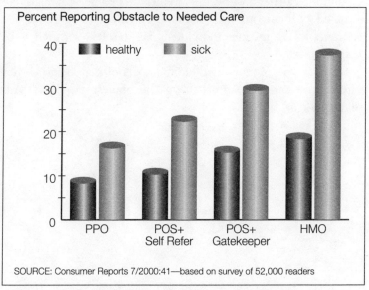

Percent Reporting Obstacle to Needed Care

SOURCE: Consumer Reports 7/2000:41—based on survey of 52,000 readers

Since most people are healthy, they have only occasional contact with their health plan, and are likely to be satisfied with care. Moreover, such healthy patients are financially attractive to managed-care plans, while the sick are unattractive. Hence, HMOs have strong incentives to tailor their services to please the healthy, and to erect barriers to care for the sick. Such barriers not only save an HMO money in the short-term, but also induce sick, unprofitable, patients to become dissatisfied and leave the plan.

Virtually every survey shows far higher levels of dissatisfaction with HMOs among sick members as compared to the healthy. Moreover, several surveys indicate that the sick have more access problems in HMOs than in fee-for-service or PPO (preferred provider option) care.

Lower income enrollees are especially dissatisfied with managed-care, according to a nationwide survey by the Commonwealth Fund. While wealthier people are relatively satisfied with care in both the managed-care and fee-for-service settings, lower income individuals are far less satisfied with managed-care.

In sum, the most vulnerable members of our society—who often need care the most—have the gravest problems with managed-care.

36. Medicaid HMOs: Poor Access and Satisfaction

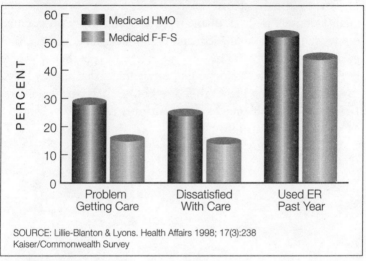

SOURCE: Lillie-Blanton & Lyons. Health Affairs 1998; 17(3):238
Kaiser/Commonwealth Survey

As just discussed, managed-care is most dangerous for vulnerable populations, and especially the poor and sick. Nonetheless, states are forcing Medicaid patients into managed-care plans. Many such plans have been hastily assembled and poorly designed. Moreover, in recent years the federal government has waived a previous requirement that Medicaid patients could be enrolled only in plans with large non-Medicaid enrollments. This requirement had been implemented after disastrous experiences in California in the 1970s. In a managed-care demonstration program under then-Governor Ronald Reagan, Medicaid-only HMOs abused thousands of poor patients, e.g., by denying them emergency care. Entrepreneurs hope to profit by setting up Medicaid HMOs and attracting healthy Medicaid patients, thus collecting the HMO premium without providing much care.

Florida was one of the first states to obtain a waiver from the federal government allowing them to opt out of fee-for-service Medicaid and enroll poor families in privately-run Medicaid HMOs. In the state's initial Medicaid managed-care program, 21 of the 29 participating plans failed to meet even minimal quality standards. In 5 plans, overhead and profits consumed more than half of total Medicaid premium dollars. Hundreds of patients reported high pressure sales tactics to get them to leave the traditional Medicaid system, e.g., threats that if they failed to sign up with the HMO they would lose their Medicaid card. Despite these problems, Florida continues to push thousands of Medicaid recipients into HMOs.

37. Satisfaction With HMOs is Falling

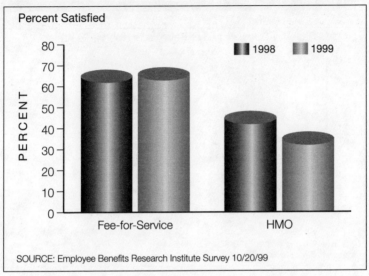

Percent Satisfied

■ 1998   ■ 1999

SOURCE: Employee Benefits Research Institute Survey 10/20/99

Patients are more satisfied with fee-for-service than managed-care, and the gap is widening. Contrary to market theory, which posits a relentless drive to improve products to attract consumers in a competitive environment, patients have become less satisfied as the HMO industry has matured. In fact, most HMOs view employers, not patients, as their real customers.

38. Elderly HMO Stroke Patients Get Less Specialist Neurology Care

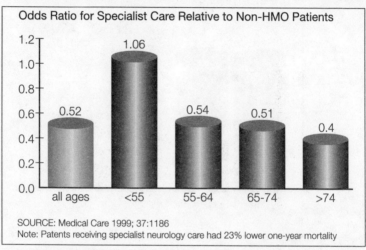

Odds Ratio for Specialist Care Relative to Non-HMO Patients

SOURCE: Medical Care 1999; 37:1186
Note: Patents receiving specialist neurology care had 23% lower one-year mortality

Neurology care from specialists has been shown to markedly improve stroke patient outcomes. This recent study analyzed patients with strokes in Minnesota. Overall, HMO patients were about half as likely as fee-for-service stroke patients to receive care from a neurology specialist. While researchers found no significant difference in the rate of specialist care among the small number of stroke patients under age 55, older HMO patients were far less likely to get such care, and the gap widened with age.

39. HMOs' Stroke Patients

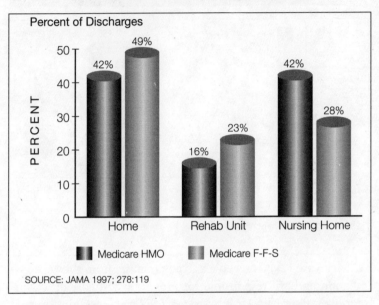

Percent of Discharges

SOURCE: JAMA 1997; 278:119

The difference in where stroke patients go when they are discharged from hospitals provides another window on the limits of HMOs. In a nationwide study of Medicare patients who suffered a stroke, HMO patients were less likely to be discharged to a rehabilitation unit or home, and more likely to be discharged to nursing homes than patients covered by traditional Medicare. A second study has confirmed this pattern. Since in most cases, the HMO is not responsible for nursing home costs, this pattern of discharges is financially favorable to the HMO, though clinically inappropriate for many patients.

40. Medicare HMO Home Care Patients: Fewer Visits, Worse Outcomes

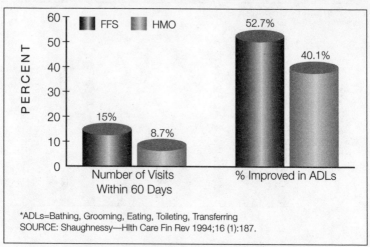

*ADLs=Bathing, Grooming, Eating, Toileting, Transferring
SOURCE: Shaughnessy—Hlth Care Fin Rev 1994;16 (1):187.

Medicare HMOs receive a fixed premium from the Medicare program and are responsible for providing virtually all care to enrollees. However, HMOs are not responsible for most nursing home costs. Hence, they have little financial incentive to provide services that would keep frail patients out of nursing homes. Medicare HMO patients receive fewer home care visits than traditional Medicare patients, and they are less likely to be able to perform activities of daily living (ADLs) independently at the conclusion of their home care. Medicare HMOs are skimping on home care, and their patient outcomes are worse as a result.

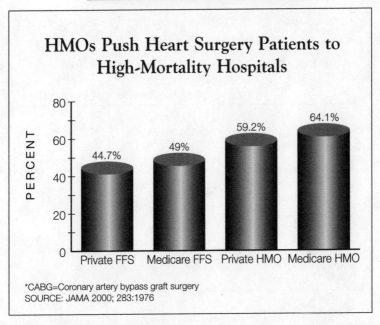

HMOs Push Heart Surgery Patients to High-Mortality Hospitals

*CABG=Coronary artery bypass graft surgery
SOURCE: JAMA 2000; 283:1976

Do HMOs select hospitals based on quality or cost? A New York State study found that HMOs selectively contract with the worst hospitals for heart surgery. Rather than directing their patients to the hospitals with the best outcomes, HMOs sent more patients to the hospitals with the highest surgical death rates.

Moreover, HMOs cannot claim ignorance about these death rates: the New York State Health Department publishes the heart surgery death rates annually. Market forces are not rewarding quality.

42. From Bad to Worse

Depressed Patients:
Fee-For-Service vs. Managed Care

	Fee-for-Service	Managed Care
Primary Care Patients		
Depression Detected	53.7%	41.8%
Appropriately Treated	60.7%	46.4%
Patients Seeing Psychiatrist		
# Functional Limitations—		
Baseline	1.3	1.5
# Functional Limitations—		
Two Years	1.2	2.0

SOURCE: Medical Outcomes Study—JAMA 1989; 262:3298 &
Arch Gen Psych 1993; 50:517

Managed care has gravely damaged the care of the mentally ill. This study compared the detection and treatment of depression in the fee-for-service setting and in four of the best HMOs in the nation. Patients cared for by HMO primary care doctors were less likely to have their depression diagnosed or appropriately treated than comparable patients cared for by fee-for-service primary care doctors. Among patients who got to see a psychiatrist, HMO members were sicker than fee-for-service enrollees. In the fee-for-service setting, the condition of patients seen by psychiatrists improved slightly. But in HMOs, during the ensuing two years, patients' clinical condition actually deteriorated.

43. Managed Mental Health: Audit Report

- Plans overstated utilization by 45%

- Delay from initial call to starting care > contractor's written standard by 97%—347%

- Plans rarely site-visited or interviewed providers

- No providers in 15% of counties "covered"; no child provider in 25% of counties

- Quality problem in 30%—58% of charts reviewed

- Criteria for inpatient care dangerously restrictive (e.g. requiring DTs prior to detox admit

- Overhead + profit NEVER consumed < 45% of premiums

SOURCE: J. Wrich—Audit findings submitted to CBO, 3/98

In recent years, a new managed mental healthcare industry has arisen. Investor-owned managed mental health firms subcontract with HMOs and employers to pay for and manage psychiatric and substance abuse care. The firms assemble a restricted group of mental health professionals authorized to provide care, excluding most skilled clinicians and threatening to "delist" providers who offer "excessive" care. To further cut costs, the firms impose restrictive utilization review. Typically, a therapist must review the patients's utilization (i.e., care) with an insurance bureaucrat empowered to authorize or prohibit further care.

Therapists report spending an hour justifying treatment for each hour they are allowed to spend with a patient. Patients, even those in the midst of a mental health crisis, may be forced to negotiate a bureaucratic maze. They often endure prolonged waits for care; and reveal the details of their distress—histories of sexual abuse, alcohol, marital, or job problems—in phone conversations with managed-care bureaucrats answerable to the patient's employers. In such circumstances, assurances of confidentiality have become meaningless.

By 2000, the ten largest managed mental healthcare firms covered 142.1 million people.

Though the patients' employers frequently hire auditors to monitor the performance of their managed mental health contractors, these audits usually remain secret. The data shown above were released to Congress in 1996, and remain the only published audit. In addition, *The Wall Street Journal* obtained data on the performance in Ohio of Biodyne, a firm subsequently known as Medco, Merit, and Magellan. Biodyne used only 34% of premiums to pay for care; the rest went for overhead and profit. In 16% of the counties covered by the contract, the firm did not have a single therapist. In one documented instance, an alcoholic was required to drive 40 minutes each way to an outpatient substance abuse clinic, and died in a drunk driving crash on his way home. Waits for care averaged 14 days. Auditors found problems in 30% of the cases they reviewed.

The overhead and profits of these managed mental health firms is staggering. Auditors have never reported overhead and profits of less than 45% of premiums.

44. Doctors Struggle to Get Care for Patients

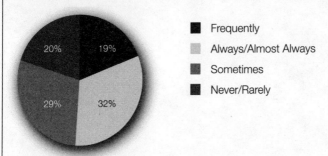

"How Often Can You Obtain High Quality Mental Health Services for Your Patients?"

- ■ Frequently
- ▨ Always/Almost Always
- ▨ Sometimes
- ■ Never/Rarely

20% 19% 29% 32%

Note: Data shown are for inpatient care; responses regarding outpatient care were similar
SOURCE: Center for Studying Health System Change, 1997—
Survey of 5,160 primary care physicians

A survey of 5,160 primary care physicians found that they are often unable to obtain needed care for their patients, especially mental healthcare. Less than one-third of physicians could always or almost always obtain satisfactory inpatient mental healthcare (as shown above). For outpatient care, only 28% of the primary care doctors said that care was always or almost always available; 16% said that care was never or rarely available.

Primary care doctors also reported problems in obtaining other kinds of needed care. 36% could not (always or almost always) obtain non-emergency hospitalizations, and 18% could not (always or almost always) refer patients to a high quality specialist. 24% of physicians said that they could not provide high quality care to all of their patients. One quarter said that they could not make clinical decisions in the best interests of their patients without reducing their incomes.

Other studies suggest that psychiatric decisions are constrained by business considerations. 64% of 2,500 psychiatrists surveyed said that their hospital set limits on length of stay, and 79% indicated that insurance companies pushed for early discharge.

45. Reducing, Not Improving, Access to Healthcare

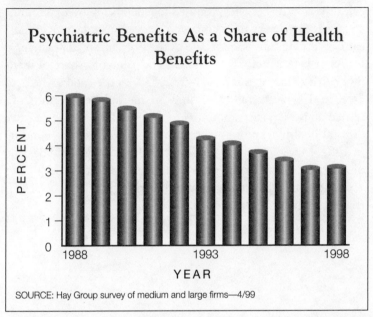

Psychiatric Benefits As a Share of Health Benefits

PERCENT

YEAR

1988 1993 1998

SOURCE: Hay Group survey of medium and large firms—4/99

Managed care has reduced access to mental healthcare, as reflected in the sharp fall in the share of employee health benefits devoted to mental health (shown above). The value of mental health benefits per "covered life," adjusted for inflation, was $154 in 1988. By 1998, that figure had fallen to $70.

The mentally ill are particularly vulnerable because they are often disinclined or unable to fight for the care they need. Many employers accept substandard care for workers with expensive-to-treat mental illnesses; poor care may force the worker to leave employment, relieving the employer of the financial burden of paying for care. For instance, most employer-sponsored plans resist paying for psychotherapy for depressed patients, despite clear evidence that depression is best treated with a combination of medication and talk therapy.

Even within the Federal Employee Health Benefits Program, mental health services' share of health spending has fallen drastically, though the benefits promised to federal employees have not changed. Managed care is changing the very paradigm of clinical care, enforcing substandard care as the only accepted practice.

As private benefits have fallen, government's share of mental health spending has risen—from 53% of the total in 1987 to 56% in 1997. Overall, spending on mental health and substance abuse services amounted to $85.3 billion in 1997, 7.8% of total health spending—down from 8.8% of health spending in 1987. Moreover, the ascendancy of drug therapy and decline of other types of treatment is striking. Prescription drug costs accounted for 7.5% of the mental health bill in 1987. By 1997, that figure had risen to 12.3%.

46. Managed Care Drives Out Charity Care

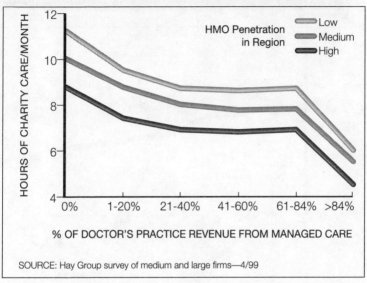

HOURS OF CHARITY CARE/MONTH

HMO Penetration in Region
- Low
- Medium
- High

% OF DOCTOR'S PRACTICE REVENUE FROM MANAGED CARE

SOURCE: Hay Group survey of medium and large firms—4/99

The effects of managed-care extend well beyond the impact on enrollees, as this and the next three charts reveal. The number of hours that doctors spend on charity care declines as the share of managed-care in their practices increase. Moreover, in areas of the country with more managed-care, doctors devote even less time to charity.

Managed care has pushed doctors to become employees of hospitals, clinics, or group practices—many of them for-profit. Often, these institutions virtually forbid physicians from seeing non-paying patients. For instance, most patients must get past a "registration" desk before even getting into a room with the doctor. Additionally, because HMOs squeeze physicians' revenues, even independent doctors are increasingly reluctant to accept non-paying patients. Finally, the business ethic that has come to dominate medicine is extinguishing charitable sentiments.

47. Eliminating Rather Than Supporting Innovation: NIH Clinical Research Grants

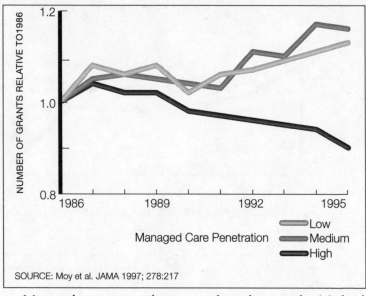

SOURCE: Moy et al. JAMA 1997; 278:217

Managed care is a threat to clinical research. Medical schools located in regions with high managed-care penetrations have received a declining share of government-sponsored clinical research grants. Notably, basic science research (which is more insulated from the pressures of managed-care) has not shown a similar pattern.

Traditionally, most clinical research has been done by faculty who spent part of their time caring for patients. But HMOs have forced increased throughput in clinics and erected barriers to part-time practice, making it more difficult to combine research with patient care. Moreover, HMOs often refuse to bear the higher costs of care at academic medical centers. While waste may account for some of these excess costs, most are due to sicker patients, better quality care, time spent on teaching, and "luxury" functions like the collegial interaction that might generate research ideas.

48. A Compromised Research Environment—Med School Deans: Managed Care Worsens

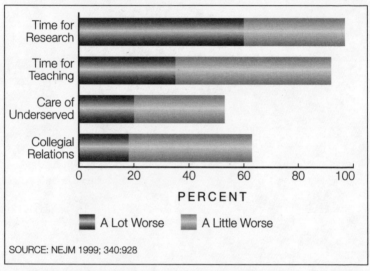

PERCENT

A Lot Worse   A Little Worse

SOURCE: NEJM 1999; 340:928

A survey of medical school deans found widespread concern that managed-care pressures are compromising the intellectual fabric of academic medicine. A separate survey of 1671 medical school faculty found an inhospitable research climate in regions with more competitive healthcare markets. Faculty cited deteriorating collegiality and conditions for research as competition increases.

49. Nurses Report More & Sicker Patients, Less Time to Teach and Comfort Them

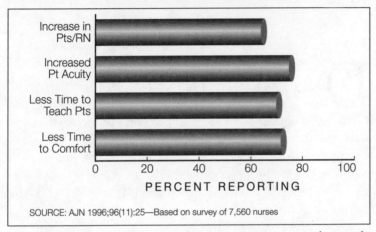

PERCENT REPORTING

SOURCE: AJN 1996;96(11):25—Based on survey of 7,560 nurses

Nurses face daunting productivity pressures as hospitals squeeze clinical budgets. In a national survey of 7,560 nurses, most reported that they were being forced to care for more and sicker patients. Nurses had less time for teaching, comforting, and other human aspects of care.

A Commonwealth Fund survey of 1710 physicians found similar problems. More than 40% of physicians reported that the amount of time available to spend with patients had been curtailed within the past three years. 20% said they had less time to keep their knowledge of medicine up to date. A rational healthcare system would deploy the surfeit of physicians to enable them to spend longer with each patient. Indeed, the most common complaint patients make about their doctor is that she/he does not spend enough time with them.

CHAPTER 5

Medicare HMOs

TAX-FUNDED PROFITEERING

Despite frequent criticisms of HMOs, both Democrats and Republicans have pushed pro-HMO policies for Medicare. Contrary to widespread perceptions, Medicare's costs have risen less than those of private insurers (where managed-care has predominated) (50). While market enthusiasts push Medicare to enroll seniors in HMOs, an AARP study found that few seniors could make informed HMO choices (51); the sickest and frailest are most vulnerable to being duped.

Currently, Medicare HMOs receive a fixed premium from Medicare for each enrollee, regardless of their health. HMOs have recruited healthier-than-average Medicare patients, and encouraged sick enrollees to disenroll when they need expensive care (52). Such strategies are highly profitable; by avoiding the sickest 4% of Medicare enrollees, a plan could avoid 46% of costs (53). This route to profitability isn't confined to health-care; a similar strategy of "cream-skimming" is emerging among for-profit charter schools (54).

50. The Inefficiency of Private Healthcare Growth in Spending 1970–1998: Medicare vs. Private Insurers

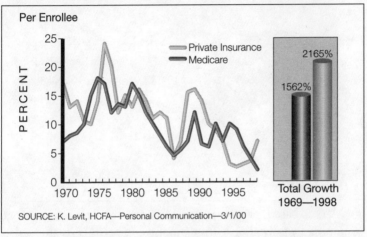

Per Enrollee

SOURCE: K. Levit, HCFA—Personal Communication—3/1/00

Market ideologues, such as George W. Bush, insist that Medicare should be reshaped to mimic private insurance—and rely on private HMOs as the middleman between government and providers. But evidence shows that strategy would be costly: Since 1970, Medicare costs have risen more slowly than private insurance costs. In the Federal Employees Health Benefit Program, which contracts with private insurers, and is cited by The Heritage Foundation and others as a market model, costs have also risen more quickly over the long run than costs have in Medicare.

By any measure, Medicare has been more efficient than private insurers. Medicare's overhead is about 2% of total spending. Overhead for private insurers, in contrast, is about 14%. And Medicare, despite covering the sickest patients in our nation, has contained costs more effectively.

51. The Fine Print

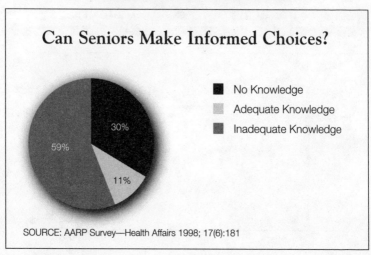

Can Seniors Make Informed Choices?

- No Knowledge
- Adequate Knowledge
- Inadequate Knowledge

30%

11%

59%

SOURCE: AARP Survey—Health Affairs 1998; 17(6):181

Market-based proposals for Medicare reform assume that seniors can wisely choose from among competing private health plans, using government vouchers. This assumption is obviously wrong for seniors with dementia or other cognitive impairments. But sorting through the fine print of health insurance contract offerings is a daunting prospect even under the best of circumstances. Weighing a $500 deductible for out-of-network specialty care against a 20% co-payment for surgery, for example, isn't straightforward.

A survey by the American Association of Retired Persons (AARP) found few seniors prepared to make informed choices about health plans. Only 11% adequately understood how HMO coverage would affect their care.

Market reform of Medicare would loose legions of insurance salesmen on America's seniors. The result is predictable: epidemic fraud, and suffering for seniors denied care.

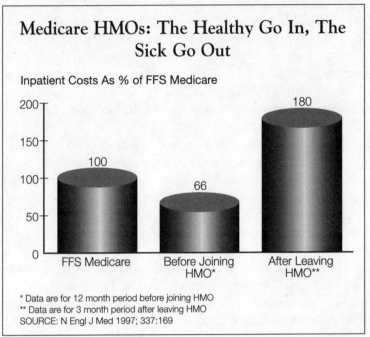

Medicare HMOs: The Healthy Go In, The Sick Go Out

Inpatient Costs As % of FFS Medicare

* Data are for 12 month period before joining HMO
** Data are for 3 month period after leaving HMO
SOURCE: N Engl J Med 1997; 337:169

Medicare pays HMOs a fee (about $700 per month in Boston) for each senior they sign up. This fee is set at 95% of the average cost of care in traditional Medicare. An HMO that enrolls healthier-than-average seniors, and encourages those who become sick to leave the HMO in order to obtain care, is virtually guaranteed a profit; though traditional Medicare would accumulate the sickest and most expensive patients.

A massive study of the records of Medicare HMO enrollees in Florida found precisely this pattern of selective enrollment and disenrollment. HMO joiners were relatively healthy; in the year before joining the HMO, they cost Medicare only 66% of what the average Medicare patient cost. Moreover, HMO patients who needed expensive care left the HMOs in large numbers (perhaps at the suggestion of their doctors who stand to lose HMO bonuses if their patients use too much care); in the three months after disenrolling, former HMO members cost traditional Medicare 180% as much as the average Medicare patient. On re-enrolling in traditional Medicare, former-HMO patients had strikingly high rates of elective surgery such as prostate surgery and hip replacement. They were 4.1 times as likely to be hospitalized for mental disorders as other Medicare patients. Some patients then reentered the HMO, but only after they had returned to good health.

As a final backstop assuring profitability, an HMO can simply pull out of any county where it's not making a profit. Most major HMOs have pulled out of at least some counties in the past three years, dumping 1.4 million seniors.

Other studies have found that HMOs enroll far healthier-than-average seniors. As compared to traditional Medicare, HMOs enroll fewer seniors who are in poor or fair health (26% vs. 18%), who need assistance with activities of daily living (14% vs. 7%), or with mental illnesses (8% vs. 4%). The Congressional Budget Office (CBO) estimates that Medicare HMOs have already increased Medicare costs by at least $2 billion annually. Just how HMOs accomplish this is discussed in chapter 6.

53. Why Cream-Skimming Works

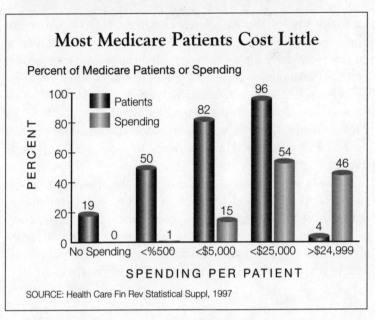

Most Medicare Patients Cost Little

Percent of Medicare Patients or Spending

Patients
Spending

PERCENT

| No Spending | <%500 | <$5,000 | <$25,000 | >$24,999 |

19 — 0 | 50 — 1 | 82 — 15 | 96 — 54 | 4 — 46

SPENDING PER PATIENT

SOURCE: Health Care Fin Rev Statistical Suppl, 1997

A relatively small number of patients incur a large proportion of medical expenses. In the Medicare program, 19% of all patients cost Medicare nothing in the course of a year, and half cost Medicare less than $500 annually—less than Medicare pays an HMO for a single month. Hence, an HMO that enrolls such people stands to profit. At the other end of the spectrum, 4% of patients incur 46% of Medicare expenditures. An HMO that avoids such patients would avoid much of the cost of care.

Moreover, it is relatively easy to sort out the profitably healthy from the unprofitably sick. One HMO published its 1992 figures on differences in patient cost. The average patient with no chronic illness cost an HMO less than $1000 annually. In contrast, patients with a diagnosis of heart disease cost $7,226, and those with a stroke $13,139. Even a diagnosis of anxiety increased average costs by 90%, and a diagnosis of arthritis, by 150%.

Finally, some HMOs have increased their profits by shifting care to VA hospitals which rarely charge the HMOs for care. At the West Los Angeles Veteran's Administration Hospital 65% of insured elderly inpatients were Medicare HMO members— but the VA collected payment for only 9% of these patients. Data from the Miami Veteran's Administration Hospital show how large a drain such a scheme can be: about two Medicare HMO members per day were admitted to the inpatient service, and 67,148 Medicare HMO patients were seen in outpatient clinics over two years.

HMO members may also receive substantial amounts of care at public hospitals and clinics that HMOs seldom reimburse, and HMO members may seek care from private physicians whose services are not covered. For instance, internal Kaiser documents suggest that members of its HMO may receive as much as 15% of their care from out-of-network providers.

54. A Transferable Profit Scheme

Risk Selection in Education

"We didn't find the academic creaming so many people worried about. What we found instead is creaming on the basis of cost. Charter schools generally are taking the students who are cheapest to educate, and leaving behind those who are more expensive."

Prof. David Arsen
U. Michigan study of charter schools

SOURCE: New York Times 10/26/99:A14

Public education may soon experience the commercial assault that medicine has suffered. Advocates for school vouchers, charter schools, and similar market-based approaches propose making billions of public dollars available to private school firms. Echoing the early history of HMOs, altruistic critics of the status quo in education have been involved in early nonprofit charter school experiments. But predictably, these nonprofit idealists will be overwhelmed in the market by entrepreneurs willing to game the system. Easy profits will accrue to schools that skim off the easiest-to-educate students, whose predictably above average test scores will fuel future arguments to expand the market.

CHAPTER 6

The HMO Scam

RICH INVESTORS, POOR CARE

As managed-care has come to dominate health insurance, for-profit HMOs have eclipsed non-profit plans (55). Yet the non-profit plans that are losing out in the marketplace rank higher on every quality measure collected by the National Committee for Quality Assurance (56). Those physicians who see more patients per hour are favored by managed-care, though they deliver worse care (57). And doctors omit needed tests and treatments for patients covered by prepaid capitation contracts that reward physicians for doing less (58). To keep costs down on complex specialty care, HMOs are increasingly pushing less costly primary care doctors to provide it, even when such care exceeds their knowledge or capabilities (59). Perhaps most disturbing, doctors face mounting pressure to avoid sick (hence unprofitable) patients (60). Even most physicians who participate in capitation payment schemes (that reward them for providing less care) believe such plans are unethical (61). HMOs sometimes explicitly forbid doctors from criticizing the plan or telling their patients how they are paid (62). More often, HMOs use the threat of "delisting " (effectively, firing) doctors who provide too much expensive care or otherwise fail to toe the corporate line (63).

Some people do well under managed-care—notably the CEOs of large healthcare firms (64). Their incomes ultimately derive from patients' premiums; overhead and profit consumes as much as one-third of premiums in the major for-profit plans (65, 66). Misbehavior in search of profit is predictable;

HMO/insurance executives owe first allegiance to their share-holders (67). To take one example of shareholder allegiance, in the 1850s, Aetna profited from slavery, and now pleads that such behavior was perfectly legal (68). More recently Cigna has deleted anti-tobacco information from subscriber newsletters at the behest of Philip Morris (69). In perhaps the clearest sign that insurance is about profit, not about health, several major insurance firms hold large investments in tobacco (70).

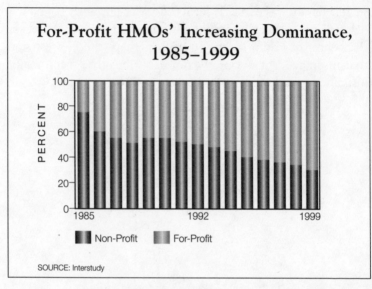

For-Profit HMOs' Increasing Dominance, 1985–1999

SOURCE: Interstudy

The recent shift to managed-care has also been a shift to investor-owned care. In 1985, three-quarters of HMO members were in non-profit plans. By 1999 only one-third of enrollees were in non-profits. Many formerly non-profit HMOs have converted to for-profit status, often enriching their executives with lucrative bonuses, consulting contracts, and stock options as part of the deal. Thus, managed-care is ushering in Wall Street's control of care.

Most research comparing HMOs with fee-for-service care has studied non-profit plans. Disturbingly, while this research has generally found similar outcomes for healthy enrollees, sick patients have fared poorly even in the best non-profit plans. Quality of care for the chronically ill in the ascendant for-profit plans is almost certainly much worse than for such patients cared for in fee-for-service settings.

56. Investor-Owned HMOs Provide Lower Quality Care

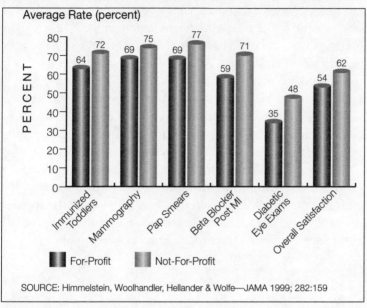

Average Rate (percent)

SOURCE: Himmelstein, Woolhandler, Hellander & Wolfe—JAMA 1999; 282:159

A Physicians for a National Health Program (PNHP) study published in the *Journal of the American Medical Association* found that investor-owned HMOs nationwide scored worse than non-profits on all 14 quality indicators reported to the National Committee for Quality Assurance. The quality measures ranged from routine preventive care (e.g., childhood immunizations, pap smears, prenatal care, and mammography) to care for patients with serious illness (e.g., eye examinations to prevent blindness in diabetics, follow-up visits for patients released from psychiatric hospitals, and prescriptions of life-saving beta blocker drugs for patients surviving heart attacks).

The largest quality differences between investor-owned and non-profit plans were in the care of seriously ill patients. As compared to non-profit plans, investor-owned HMOs had a 27% lower rate of eye examinations for diabetics; a 23% lower rate of beta blocker use for heart attack survivors; and a 9% lower rate of follow-up for patients released from mental hospitals. Rates for childhood immunizations were 12% lower; for pap smears, 9% lower; and for mammography, 8% lower in investor-owned plans. The study calculated that if all American women were enrolled in for-profit HMOs instead of non-profits, the annual death toll from breast cancer would rise by 5,925.

While costs in investor-owned and non-profit plans were similar ($128 per member, per month, vs. $127.50), investor-owned plans spent 48% more on administration and profits (19.4% of revenues vs. 13.1%), and less for patient care.

For-profits also have a dismal record on another indicator of quality, the proportion of Medicare patients who choose to disenroll from the HMO. Seven of the 10 plans with the highest disenrollment rates were investor-owned, while 9 of the 10 plans with the lowest disenrollment rates were non-profit.

57. Productive Physicians, Worse Care

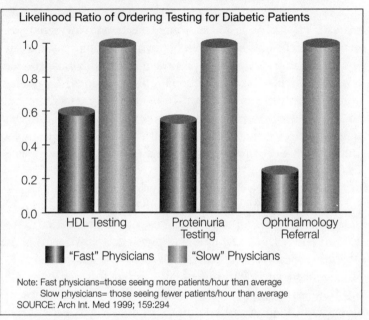

Likelihood Ratio of Ordering Testing for Diabetic Patients

HDL Testing   Proteinuria Testing   Ophthalmology Referral

■ "Fast" Physicians   ■ "Slow" Physicians

Note: Fast physicians=those seeing more patients/hour than average
Slow physicians= those seeing fewer patients/hour than average
SOURCE: Arch Int. Med 1999; 159:294

Physicians seeing more patients per hour ("fast" physicians) are less likely to provide appropriate care to their diabetic patients—blood tests for HDL cholesterol; urine testing for kidney function; or referral for a thorough eye exam.

Fast throughput is highly valued by the private employers [who pay for workers' insurance] who managed-care plans increasingly view as "the customer." Employers define optimal care as minimized costs, high worker productivity, and maximum leverage over employees—strike and you lose your healthcare. HMOs win contracts by promising employers the modern version of the company doctor—willing to squeeze care, avoid embarrassing diagnoses of workplace-induced illnesses, and equate quality with lowered absenteeism.

These imperatives undermine much that is rational and desirable in doctor-patient interactions. Patients want from their doctors more time; more information; more mutuality in decision making, therapy and prevention; and more caring. Instead, HMOs press for shortened visits and increased volume—amidst a nationwide glut of physicians. Empathy, humanity, imagination are neither profitable nor readily quantifiable, and as U.S. Healthcare's billionaire CEO opined, "It doesn't count unless you can count it." Instead managers measure care in the false coin of throughput, short-term satisfaction, and quality indices such as HEDIS (Health Plan Employer Data and Information Set) that assess tiny and easily manipulated slices of clinical life.

Doctors who see fewer patients—who are, in the language of managed-care "unproductive"—involve patients more in decision making. This, in turn correlates with higher patient satisfaction and with less switching of physicians. Physicians' sense of autonomy and a long duration of the doctor/patient relationship are associated with these same positive features.

Time is needed to search for needs rather than merely satisfying immediate wants; educate both doctor and patient, and involve them as co-producers. Only time will allow doctors to engage the social and psychological problems that most patients have, not just rule out the biological problems they don't have. Good care can be sparing of everything but time.

58. Incentives for Doctors to Withhold Care

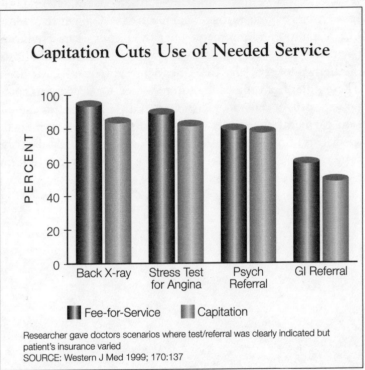

Capitation Cuts Use of Needed Service

Researcher gave doctors scenarios where test/referral was clearly indicated but patient's insurance varied
SOURCE: Western J Med 1999; 170:137

HMOs are tethering physicians' incomes to behaviors that further corporate profitability. In 1987 most HMOs paid physicians straight salaries. By 1996, 74% of independent practice associations (IPAs) and 50% of group/staff model HMOs based physicians' payment in part on utilization (i.e., cost) measures. If doctors save money on costs, they receive higher pay. A raft of data confirms that doctors respond to such incentives by decreasing care—both necessary and unnecessary. In the study shown above, researchers gave physicians case scenarios in which a test or referral was clearly needed. When the scenario stated that the patient's insurer paid on a capitation basis, doctors recommended fewer of these medically necessary tests/referrals.

A variety of payment schemes have been devised that reward doctors for restricting care—in some cases, offering utilization-based bonuses that could reach $150,000 per year. Most U.S. capitation arrangements offer the primary care physician payments that cover not only their own work, but also the costs of referrals for specialty care, inpatient care, or other services. These differ from the capitation fees used for decades to compensate British general practitioners (GPs). The British capitation payments cover only the work of the GP, not referrals to specialists or other services. Thus, the incentives under British-style capitation are weaker than under the "at risk" capitation systems now prevalent in the U.S.

59. Primary Care Doctors Are Pushed to Provide Complex Care Without Specialists

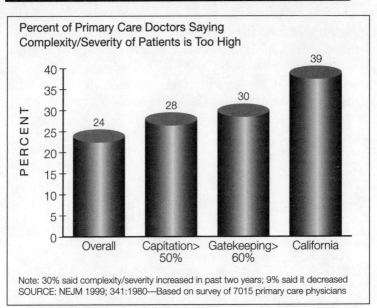

Percent of Primary Care Doctors Saying Complexity/Severity of Patients is Too High

Note: 30% said complexity/severity increased in past two years; 9% said it decreased
SOURCE: NEJM 1999; 341:1980—Based on survey of 7015 primary care physicians

It's hard to be a good doctor. The ways we are paid often distort our clinical and moral judgment, and seldom improve it. The more extreme the financial incentives, the more extreme will be the distortions. Capitation and similar payment schemes discourage primary care doctors from referring patients with complex problems to specialists, as illustrated above.

In some fee-for-service arrangements physicians received bonuses or profits for prescribing care delivered by others (e.g., x-rays and hospitalizations). The practice was banned by Federal and state "anti-kickback" statutes. But these banned kickbacks are the ethical equivalent and mirror image of incentives doctors receive for withholding care.

Financial incentives are not necessary for cost control and are expensive to administer. A single payer system like Canada's (in which taxes support a health insurance program covering everyone), limits entrepreneurial rewards and penalties, covers all, and saves money on bureaucracy and profits. The public budgetary ceilings that constrain costs bring doctors and patients into conflict with budget setters (and taxpayers); but not with each other. In a Canadian-style system, the doctor is not penalized if she consults other doctors when caring for patients with complex medical problems.

60. Money Changes Everything

Doctors Urged to Shun the Sick

"[We can] no longer tolerate patients with complex and expensive-to-treat conditions being encouraged to transfer to our group."

Letter to faculty from University of California Irvine Hospital chief

SOURCE: Modern Healthcare, 9/21/95: 172.

Increasingly, HMOs grant caregivers and patients access to each other only so long as their relationship profits the HMO. Most managed-care plans engage in "economic profiling," assessments of doctors' contribution to profitability, and base practitioner income (at least partially) on these profiles. Since most managed-care contracts allow the firm to fire practitioners "without cause," HMOs can terminate unprofitable doctor-patient dyads.

Capitation and bonus systems reward physicians who care for healthier patients. This pressures doctors to exploit patients' trust for financial gain. Physicians can influence patients' health plan choices, and know patients' health status and care-seeking behavior—the optimal data for risk selection. Doctors who triage healthy, low-cost seniors to a Medicare HMO and sick ones to traditional Medicare get windfall profits from the former and continued revenues from the latter (whose bills will be paid by traditional Medicare on a fee-for-service basis). HMOs already illegally query 43% of Medicare applicants about their health status when they apply for membership, though Medicare regulations prohibit such pre-enrollment inquiries.

Policing exam room conversations is far harder. The net effect: healthy seniors (and their Medicare dollars) migrate to profitable HMOs, leaving sicker patients in traditional Medicare. As noted earlier, the Congressional Budget Office estimates that this adds $2 billion per year in total costs.

Doctors who attract sick patients—e.g., experienced surgeons, minority physicians, medical school faculty, and those caring for the poor—risk being red-lined in the new medical marketplace. For instance, patients of minority physicians have a larger number of severe symptoms (1.33 vs. 1.14 symptoms), concurrent medical problems (1.3 vs. 1.1), and functional limitations (1.57 vs. 1.32) than the patients of white physicians.

61. Most Physicians Believe Capitation is Unethical, Including Those Paid Capitation

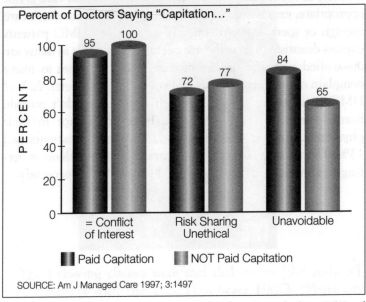

Percent of Doctors Saying "Capitation..."

- **Paid Capitation**
- **NOT Paid Capitation**

SOURCE: Am J Managed Care 1997; 3:1497

This survey suggests that many physicians, including 95% of those who receive capitation payments, believe that these incentives to withhold care create an inherent conflict of interest.

A separate survey of primary care physicians in 89 California group practices found physicians less satisfied with all aspects of care for capitated patients than for other patients in their practice. 88% of physicians were very or somewhat satisfied with relationships with patients in their overall practice, vs. 71% with capitated patients. 88% were satisfied with the quality of care overall, vs. 64% for capitated patients. 79% were satisfied overall with their ability to treat patients according to their best judgment vs. 51% for capitated patients; and 59% were satisfied

tract still included a requirement that physicians not "imply to members that their care or access to care will be inferior due to the source of payment" (Aetna U.S. Healthcare physician contract, October, 1998). Moreover, virtually every HMO contract includes a clause allowing the HMO to terminate any physician without cause. Such termination-at-will clauses, like gag clauses, discourage physicians from publicly criticizing the plan.

What are HMOs hiding? Plans have discovered that bureaucratic efforts to limit care are far less effective than giving physicians "bribes" to limit care, or imposing steep penalties when they lose money for the HMO. Such arrangements disturb patients, as well as physicians. Hence the need to impose silence.

63. We Select Your Doctors

Recently, United Healthcare HMO announced plans to drop most of its utilization review requirements, allegedly giving physicians free rein to order expensive care. But the move, which played with great fanfare in the media, is more illusory than substantive: United Healthcare retained the power to terminate physicians who spent too much.

64. CEO Pay and Stockholdings, 1998

CEO	Firm	Pay	Stock
Wilson Taylor	*Cigna*	$7.5 million	$125.3 million
William McGuire	*United Hlthcr.*	$4.8 million	$243.7 million
Norman Payson	*Oxford*	$4.5 million	$57.2 million
Leonard Shaeffer	*Wellpoint*	$3.3 million	$62.6 million
David Jones	*Humana*	$1.0 million	$74.1 million
Fred Hassan	*Pharmacia Upjohn*	$15.1 million	$120.9 million
Melvin Goodes	*Warner Lambert*	$11.8 million	$307.3 million
Richard Scrushy	*Health South*	$3.0 million	$106.0 million
Thomas Frist Jr.	*Columbia/HCA*	$.032 million	$504.9 million

SOURCE: Jenks Healthcare Business Report 9/24/00 and SEC Filings.
Stock holdings based on stock prices as of 12/31/99.

Some people have done well in managed-care, e.g., HMO Chief Executive Officers—the first 5 listed on the chart above. Leonard Abramson, probably the wealthiest of all HMO executives, is not listed because he recently sold his interest in U.S. Healthcare to Aetna, and is no longer the CEO of that firm (he remains the largest stockholder). Mr. Abramson netted $990 million from his stockholdings in U.S. Healthcare, and was allowed to keep his corporate jet in the deal.

Also listed on this chart are some high-paid executives of drug, nursing home, medical device, and hospital firms. In 1998, the CEOs of 10 drug companies averaged $20 million in compensation. Together they held more than $1 billion in stock options.

65. HMO Overhead and Profits

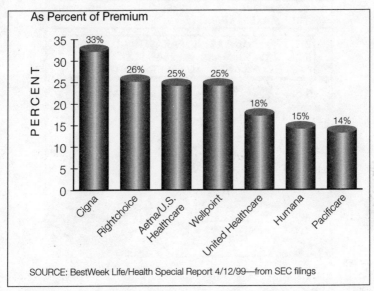

As Percent of Premium

SOURCE: BestWeek Life/Health Special Report 4/12/99—from SEC filings

The average HMO takes 13%–19% of total premiums for overhead and profits. However, the most financially successful HMO's have higher than average overhead, sometimes as high as 33%. Stock prices generally rise when HMOs report that their "loss ratios" (the amount of premium spent on medical care) falls. In contrast, administration consumes about 2% of Medicare costs. In Canada's national health insurance program, administration costs just 0.9%.

66. Free Markets

IF YOU BELIEVE THAT A FREE-MARKET INSURANCE SYSTEM MAKES *SENSE*...

WELL OF *COURSE* A PARASITICAL MIDDLE-MAN HAS TO MAKE A PROFIT BEFORE I CAN BE ALLOWED ACCESS TO HEALTH CARE!

IT'S THE AMERICAN WAY!

TOM TOMORROW © 6-3-98

67. Corporate Social Responsibility?

> "Few trends could so thoroughly undermine the very foundations of our free society as the acceptance by corporate officials of a social responsibility other than to make as much money for their shareholders as possible."
>
> —Milton Friedman

SOURCE: Milton Friedman—Capitalism & Freedom, 1962.

The leading academic advocate of free market economics, Milton Friedman, argues that the market has no room for social responsibility. Financial considerations govern the actions of corporate officials. Indeed, by law, executives' primary fiduciary duty is to their shareholders.

For-profit hospitals offer a case study in the conflict between profit-maximization and social responsibility. For-profit hospitals have high death rates and high costs, as detailed on several subsequent pages. The two largest for-profit hospital firms— HCA—The Healthcare Company (formerly Columbia/HCA) and Tenet (formerly National Medical Enterprises)—demonstrate the lengths to which companies will go in the quest to enrich shareholders: Both have been implicated in massive fraud. Unlike HMOs, hospital firms generally profit by increasing utilization, then billing insurers for the maximum amount possible.

Columbia/HCA grew rapidly during the 1990s to become the largest for-profit hospital firm. By 1996 it had total revenues of $19.9 billion and pre-tax profits of $2.66 billion from 343 hospitals, 136 outpatient surgery centers and about 550 home healthcare agencies. It appears that fraudulent or questionable practices were an important part of Columbia's business strategy.

The New York Times unearthed extensive evidence that Columbia systematically falsified cost reports filed with the Federal government in order to inflate Medicare billings. For instance, the Medicare hospital payment system has several categories for pneumonia. Billing under the highest category (meant to cover the sickest pneumonia patients) brings a hospital $3,650 more per case than billing under the least complex category. Columbia's hospitals almost always billed for the most complex pneumonia category. At Cedars Columbia Hospital, which Columbia purchased in 1992, the proportion of cases billed at the most complex level grew dramatically the year after Columbia's purchase. In contrast, the public hospital next door showed no such increase in severity of illness. Overall, Columbia billed Medicare for a 15% sicker case-mix than other acute care hospitals, yet had an average length of stay that was 10% shorter.

Columbia also inflated its profits by referring Medicare patients to Columbia-owned home-care and other post-acute services. Thus, Columbia would collect the fixed Medicare payment for the acute inpatient stay, then refer patients for extensive post-acute care that could be billed to Medicare on a fee-for-service basis. As a result, Medicare costs in the 30 days after discharge for patients in Texas averaged $3,627 for Columbia's patients, and only $2,900 for patients treated at public and non-for-profit hospitals.

When press coverage reveals fraud as massive as that at Columbia, it's tempting to view it as the isolated result of a few bad apples. But other for-profit hospitals also had very high post-acute costs, suggesting that Columbia's practices were not unique and may be common in for-profit hospitals.

Columbia encouraged physicians to invest money in its hospitals, giving the physicians financial incentives to refer well-insured patients to the Columbia-owned facilities. It pressured administrators and physicians not to admit the uninsured; and offered administrators bonuses that amounted to more than 80% of their salaries if the hospital's profits were high. Executives whose hospitals were less profitable were denied bonuses and sometimes forced out altogether. Columbia also sought profits by squeezing its own workers; the company was also convicted of unfair labor practices and intimidation of employees who were attempting to organize a union.

In buying non-profit institutions, Columbia offered large financial incentives to non-profit executives who cooperated. For instance, when Columbia sought to purchase Blue Cross of Ohio, it offered John Burry, Jr., the Chairman and CEO, consulting agreements that would net him up to $7 million, as well as $3 million for agreeing to a no-compete contract. Other Blue Cross executives were also offered lucrative deals.

On several occasions Columbia closed essential community health facilities because they were not profitable. While it was squeezing clinical services in order to increase profitability, the company was spending enormous amounts on advertising; $85 million in 1995; $106 million in 1996 ($1,567 per bed). One of its advertisements falsely claimed that the company had been awarded the Malcolm Baldridge Award for quality.

The second largest firm, Tenet, has paid more than $600 million in fines and legal settlements for its activities. Starting in the mid-1980's, Tenet/NME paid kickbacks for referrals of patients to its psychiatric hospitals, and in some cases virtually kidnapped patients and held them against their will in order to keep psychiatric beds full. Despite a pattern of insurance fraud, payment of kickbacks, and charges of bribing state officials, Tenet has continued to grow and prosper.

68. Then as Now:
Aetna and Slave Insurance

A rider to Aetna's slave policies indicates that the firm knew the horrors of slave life. It excluded payments in cases where slaves were lynched, worked to death, or committed suicide. Though slavery is outlawed today, the underlying structure governing corporate choices remains constant: investor-owned firms predictably exploit immoral profit opportunities.

Individuals who have amassed extreme wealth from the misfortune of others, and corporations that insure slave owners deserve scorn and rebuke. Yet it's important to understand that in a competitive system, companies are compelled to commit legal, but immoral acts. Had Aetna not offered slave insurance, it might not have survived to the 20th century, losing out to competitors willing to write such policies. Market competition stimulates such immoral acts. Today, healthcare companies that shy away from egregious practices (e.g., denying expensive care to the seriously ill) risk driving investors to competitors with fewer scruples and larger profits.

Real change requires more than admonishing firms to have a social conscience. We must change the system that pushes corporations to act irresponsibly. In the case of healthcare, only a tax-funded, non-profit system can reverse murderous incentives.

69. Cigna Censored Anti-Tobacco Messages At Philip Morris' Request

"We worked with Cigna to take out some of the references in the [health] newsletters that we thought could be offensive or annoying to our employees."

Philip Morris Spokesperson

"Philip Morris was paying for a product...We work with our customers to try to help them meet their business needs."

Cigna Spokesperson

SOURCE: Minneapolis Star Tribune 2/4/2000

Cigna, the current market leader among for-profit HMOs, frequently deleted or altered stories with anti-tobacco messages in its health newsletters at the behest of the Philip Morris Tobacco Company. The newsletters were sent to Cigna health plan enrollees who were employed by Philip Morris, which includes Kraft Foods and Miller Beer.

Company emails that came to light as part of a lawsuit against tobacco firms reveal that Cigna routinely consulted Philip Morris officials about the newsletter's contents, and discussed how to minimize references to the hazards of smoking in articles about asthma, heart disease, pregnancy, ear infections, and even safe behavior around lawn mowers. Cigna employees rewrote some articles at Philip Morris' behest. In other cases articles were removed.

Cigna withheld at least two issues of the newsletter from Philip Morris employees: one issue included several articles referring to the dangers of smoking, as well as an advertisement for a video series featuring former Surgeon General (and anti-smoking advocate) Dr. C. Everett Koop; the second censored issue informed readers that secondhand smoke can trigger asthma.

The Cigna spokesperson quoted above makes it clear Cigna's customer is not the patient but the employer who foots the bill. When they conflict, as they do here, the insurer puts the employer's needs ahead of the employee's health concern.

70. Health Insurers' Tobacco Stock

Stock Holdings in 1999—$ Millions

	Prudential	MetLife/Travelers	Cigna
RJ Reynolds	$137.2	—	—
Philip Morris	$435.2	$55.3	$38.6
Loews (Kent etc.)	$319.6	$6.8	$4.1

SOURCE: Boyd, Himmelstein & Woolhandler—JAMA 8/9/2000

Large insurance firms, who are among the largest owners of for-profit HMOs, are also major investors in tobacco. Insurers are in business to make profits, with little concern for health. We liken this investment to the combined taxidermy and veterinarian shop: either way you get your dog back.

CHAPTER 7

Corporate Care

INFERIOR QUALITY, INFLATED PRICES

Other firms besides HMOs that profit from care have also demonstrated a flexible sense of morality. The consulting firm whose guidelines are used by many HMOs to dictate lengths of hospital stays suggests dangerously brief hospitalizations for seriously ill children (71). The firm apparently demands little proof that its guidelines are safe, as long as they are "efficient" (72). Meanwhile for-profit ownership is spreading in many sectors of healthcare delivery (73), and massive fraud has become routine (74).

The two largest investor-owned hospital chains have admitted to illegal schemes to pad their incomes. But even when not engaged in unlawful behavior, for-profit hospitals cost more and provide worse care. In communities whose medical market is dominated by investor-owned hospitals, health costs are higher and rising faster than in areas dominated by non-profits (75). Much of the excess costs of for-profit hospitals are due to higher administrative costs; they actually spend less on clinical personnel than do non-profits (76). Death rates at for-profit hospitals are 7% higher than at comparable non-profit hospitals (77) and have been for at least a decade (78). Other studies confirm this disturbing finding (79), and suggest that inadequate nurse staffing at investor-owned hospitals causes postoperative complications (80).

Poor quality has also become endemic among other types of for-profit health facilities. Nursing homes, most of which are investor-owned, have been plagued by low quality care and chronically poor staffing (81). For-profit dialysis clinics have high death rates, low transplant rates (82), and less use of the optimal type of dialysis (peritoneal) for children (83). Canadian dialysis clinics, virtually all of them non-profit, provide better care at lower cost (84). In sum, investor-owned health facilities provide inferior care at inflated prices (85).

71. Cutting Costs to the Bone

Milliman & Robertson Pediatric Length of Stay Guidelines

- 1 Day for Diabetic Coma
- 2 Days for Osteomyelitis
- 3 Days for Bacterial Meningitis

"They're outrageous. They're dangerous. Kids could die because of these guidelines."

Thomas Cleary, M.D.
Prof. of Pediatrics, U. Texas, Houston
Listed as "Contributing Author" in M&R manual

SOURCE: Modern Healthcare May 8, 2000:34

Milliman and Robertson (M&R) is an actuarial firm that produces length-of-stay guidelines used by thousands of U.S. hospitals and managed-care plans providing care to tens of millions of patients. Several of their recent pediatrics guidelines are shown above.

M&R listed Dr. Thomas Cleary as a "Contributing Author" of the guidelines after M&R gave his department $100,000. He and other physicians listed as authors have since dissociated themselves from the guidelines.

Adult M&R guidelines (as reported in *The New York Times* in 1995) have included restrictions on: 1) having cataracts removed from more than one eye unless the patient is young and needs both eyes to work; 2) staying overnight for a mastectomy; 3) staying more than one day for a vaginal delivery or more than two days for a caesarean; 4) seeing a neurologist for new onset seizures; and 5) staying more than 3 days for a stroke, even if the patient can't walk.

72. Corporate Healthcare Guidelines: Economics, Not Science

We Do Not Base Our Guidelines...

"We do not base our guidelines on any randomized clinical trials or other controlled studies, nor do we study outcomes before sharing the evidence of most efficient practices with colleagues."

Milliman & Robertson
Wall Street Journal 7/1/98

Consulting firms often arrive at guidelines recommending the length of a hospital stay by analyzing accounting data, with little or no attention to how patients actually fared. They typically identify a few patients with a given diagnosis who were discharged very quickly. The consultants presume that such short stays are OK for virtually all patients with this diagnosis, and prescribe quick discharges as the most efficient care. But they ignore the clinical reality that patients who share a diagnosis may differ radically. For instance, a patient whose stroke leaves them with only slight weakness in one side of their face might appropriately go home quickly, while someone with the same diagnosis who suffers loss of speech, paralysis, and swallowing difficulties would require a much longer stay.

Apparently, M&R does not actually study the outcomes of patients affected by its guidelines.

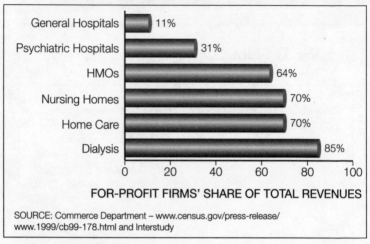

73. Extent of For-Profit Ownership, 1998

General Hospitals — 11%
Psychiatric Hospitals — 31%
HMOs — 64%
Nursing Homes — 70%
Home Care — 70%
Dialysis — 85%

FOR-PROFIT FIRMS' SHARE OF TOTAL REVENUES

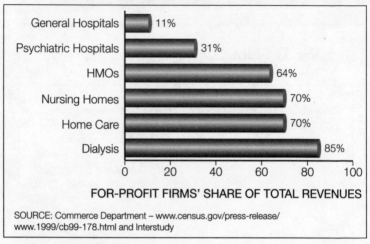

SOURCE: Commerce Department – www.census.gov/press-release/
www.1999/cb99-178.html and Interstudy

The United States is unique in allowing for-profit firms to dominate major sectors of healthcare delivery.

Traditionally, medicine was operated as a public service by government or charities, like education, road building, and water and sewage systems. Healthcare was necessary for the profitability of other industries—and for social stability—but was not an important source of profit-making. Only recently has medicine become not only a service for the rest of industry and society but a major profit-producing industry in its own right.

74. Profit-Driven Care Begets Fraud

Recent Criminal and Civil Fines/Settlements

- **NME** (Tenet)—$683 million: Medicare fraud, patient abuse
- SmithKline, Corning, LabCorp—>$800 million: Billing fraud
- **Caremark**—>$200 million: Kickbacks & fraud in home IV business
- Fresenius/NMC—$486 million: Dialysis fraud
- **Roche & BASF**—>$725 million: Price fixing cartel
- Beverly—$175 million: Nursing home fraud
- Noll—$135 million: Suppressing research data on Synthroid
- **Abbott Labs**—$100 million: Faulty lab test kits
- **Columbia/HCA**—$745 million fraud and continuing investigation

SOURCE: NY Times 7/30/97, 10/10/99, 11/3/99, 1/20/00, 2/4/00; Modern Healthcare 3/25/96, 3/3/97; Nation 4/7/97; DHHS Insp. Genl.; CBS 60 Minutes 12/19/99

Large-scale medical fraud has become routine as for-profit firms have gained a foothold in the healthcare system. This chart displays some recent large settlements and fines paid by healthcare firms. In addition, the U.S. General Accounting Office has estimated that about 25% of all home care agencies (most of which are for-profit) defraud Medicare.

HMO patient protection acts and similar regulatory approaches merely embellish the cops and robbers game that has become the central focus of healthcare. Market-driven health policies have offered billions of dollars to entrepreneurs who cheat patients out of care, and taxpayers out of Medicare dollars. Each new round of market incentives breeds new abuses and then new regulations. Each round adds a new army of bureaucrats; thousands of regulators and tens of thousands working to skirt the regulations.

Healthcare entrepreneurs routinely circumvent existing regulations. It's already a Federal offense for HMOs to selectively recruit healthy seniors, or to evict the sick—yet they continue the practice. Hospitals pay kickbacks for referrals; drug and device firms suppress research data, inflate the benefits and hide the risk of their products; and a panoply of firms that bill Medicare falsely inflate their billings.

The owners of profit-driven health firms have discovered, to their advantage, that you can't legislate good medical care: that subtle mix of science, psychology, intuition, and kindness; rife with judgment calls in the face of scientific uncertainty. After 15 years of market medicine, costs are climbing, coverage is crumbling; avarice is ascendant.

All societies exclude some realms from the market's reach. Because human blood that's sold is more likely to be tainted, we rely on donations for our transfusions. We proscribe the selling of children for adoption or organs for transplantation. We do not leave fire or police departments, or the military, to the mercy of the market. Imagine a fire department that demanded proof that the homeowner could pay for services prior to visiting a burning home. Imagine further that the fire department made more money every time it refused to intervene, and provided poorer firefighting as a cost-saving maneuver. Would the firefighters arrive, intent on scrimping on water? Or, perhaps, they might save only the living room and admonish the homeowner to look elsewhere for more comprehensive help, all the while proclaiming how great such a free-market fire system is. These images are outrageous to the point of being comical. Yet they have parallels in our healthcare system. No other nation has ceded healthcare to investors; none save us needs laws to protect patients from their caregivers.

75. Medicare Costs Rose Faster in Communities with For-Profit Hospitals

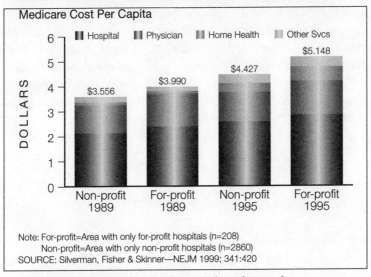

Medicare Cost Per Capita

Note: For-profit=Area with only for-profit hospitals (n=208)
      Non-profit=Area with only non-profit hospitals (n=2860)
SOURCE: Silverman, Fisher & Skinner—NEJM 1999; 341:420

The dogma of market medicine, that the profit motive optimizes care and minimizes costs, seems impervious to evidence.

Studies have shown for decades that for-profit hospitals are 3%–11% more expensive than non-profits; no peer-reviewed study has found the opposite. For-profit rehabilitation facilities are also costlier than non-profits, charging Medicare $4,888 more per admission.

Investor-owned hospitals also raise costs outside their walls. The data shown above indicate that in areas where investor-owned hospitals dominate the market, Medicare pays more, not only for hospital care, but for home care and care in other facilities as well. These cost differences widened between 1989 and 1995. A switch to for-profit ownership coincided with a spurt in Medicare spending. The high cost of for-profit hospitals robbed Medicare of $5.2 billion in 1995. By extrapolation, had all U.S.

hospitals been for-profit, Medicare's annual tab would have been $24.3 billion higher than had there been no for-profits.

In areas with a mix of for-profit and non-profit hospitals, costs are intermediate. Perhaps this reflects an average of high cost for-profit hospitals and cheaper non-profits. But more likely, non-profits emulate for-profits when forced to compete with them; e.g., matching Columbia/HCA's marketing budget of $1,567 per bed, or offering perks to physicians. Among psychiatric hospitals for example, non-profits provide more free care than for-profits in noncompetitive markets, but in competitive markets their behavior converges and free care falls.

76. Why Are For-Profit Hospitals Costlier?

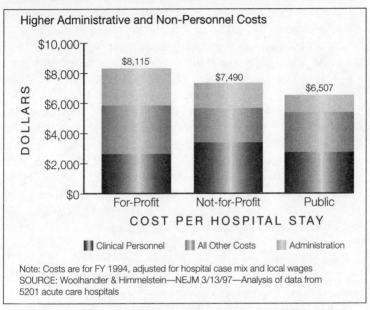

Higher Administrative and Non-Personnel Costs

COST PER HOSPITAL STAY

■ Clinical Personnel   ▨ All Other Costs   ▨ Administration

Note: Costs are for FY 1994, adjusted for hospital case mix and local wages
SOURCE: Woolhandler & Himmelstein—NEJM 3/13/97—Analysis of data from
5201 acute care hospitals

For-profit hospitals spend less on personnel, avoid charity care, and shorten stays. But because they spend far more on administration and ancillary services, their total costs are higher.

Our analysis of Medicare data for virtually every U.S. hospital found 8% higher costs per hospital stay at for-profit hospitals than at non-profit hospitals, and an even bigger difference between for-profit and public hospitals. Most of the difference was accounted for by the much higher costs of administration at for-profit hospitals. Administrative costs per hospital discharge averaged $2,289 at for-profit hospitals, $1,809 at not-for-profit hospitals, and $1,432 at public hospitals.

For-profit hospitals spent less on clinical personnel than not-for-profit hospitals. Indeed, wage and salary costs accounted for only 40.9% of total costs at for-profit hospitals, vs. 48% at not-for-profit and public hospitals. Employee benefit costs were also lower at for-profit hospitals, 6.7% of total costs vs. 8.1% at not-for-profit and public hospitals.

How does investor ownership increase costs? Successful for-profit executives reap princely rewards, raising their personal stake in gaming the payment system. When Columbia's CEO, Richard Scott, resigned in the face of federal fraud investigations, he left with a $10 million severance package and $269 million in company stock. Thomas Frist, who was the Chairman and CEO of HCA before it merged with Columbia, and succeeded Mr. Scott after he was ousted as Columbia's head, was the highest-paid executive in the United States in 1992, receiving $127 million. And these two were not the only big winners among Columbia's executives. In 1992 alone, Paul McKnight, a Senior Vice President, received $7.86 million; Joseph DiLorenzo received $12 million; Donald Fish received $10.5 million; and Jack Bovender received $9.8 million. Incentive bonuses averaged 41.5% of administrators' pay at for-profit hospitals vs. 19.7% at non-profits. In 1995, 25% of Columbia's administrators received profit-related bonuses of at least 80% of their salaries; many who didn't were forced out for not making enough profits for shareholders.

Like Columbia, Tenet and NME executives have been handsomely rewarded. For instance, in the mid-1980's NME executives (who presided over the company's fraudulent activities) were the highest paid executives in Los Angeles. In 1991, Richard Eamer, NME's Chief Executive, who later resigned in disgrace after the company's illegal activities were unearthed, made $17.5 million, number five on the Forbes list of best-paid CEOs.

Contrary to arguments touting profitability as an incentive to improve efficiency, strategies that bolster profitability often worsen efficiency. Columbia hospitals apparently inflated Medicare billings by upcoding DRGs (diagnoses that determine Medicare payments), falsifying Medicare Cost Reports, and augmenting referrals to affiliated home care agencies and sub-acute facilities.

Investor-owned hospitals are profit maximizers, not cost minimizers.

77. Death Rates Are Higher at For-Profit Hospitals

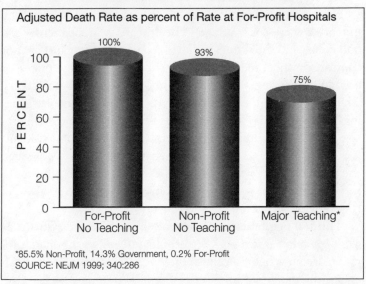

Adjusted Death Rate as percent of Rate at For-Profit Hospitals

*85.5% Non-Profit, 14.3% Government, 0.2% For-Profit
SOURCE: NEJM 1999; 340:286

A 1999 New England Journal of Medicine study found that death rates for seriously-ill Medicare patients were 7% lower at non-profit, non-teaching hospitals than at comparable for-profit hospitals; teaching hospitals, virtually all of them non-profit, had 25% lower death rates. The research examined deaths among patients hospitalized with hip fracture, stroke, congestive heart failure, or coronary heart disease. Total Medicare costs over six months averaged $13,003 per patient at for-profit non-teaching hospitals, $12,735 at teaching hospitals, and $11,765 at non-profit, non-teaching hospitals.

Why doesn't the market weed out firms offering inferior products at inflated prices?

The simplest explanation is that the competitive free market described in textbooks does not, and cannot, exist in healthcare. First, many hospitals exercise virtual monopolies. As previously noted, roughly half of Americans live in areas too sparsely populated to support medical competition. For-profit chains have concentrated their hospital purchases in locales where they can control much of the market.

Second, informed consumer choice, the driver of efficiency in market theory, is a mirage in healthcare. Many patients (e.g. frail elders and the seriously ill who consume most care) cannot comparison shop, reduce demand when suppliers raise prices, or accurately appraise quality. Patients rely on their caregivers' advice. Even lucid, educated patients may have difficulty gauging whether a 7-day hospital stay is better than the more lucrative (for the hospital) alternative of a 2-day hospital stay followed by 12 days in a hospital-owned nursing facility. Moreover, the product isn't sold to the healthcare consumer but rather to the employer who pays the bill; consumers have little power of the wallet.

Third, if purchasers can't accurately appraise a product they can't set a fair price; efforts to evaluate care are no match for profit-driven schemes to misrepresent it. Doctors and hospitals create the data used to monitor them. When used as the basis for financial reward such data has the accuracy of a tax return. By labeling minor chest discomfort "angina" rather than "chest pain" a hospital can raise its Medicare payment 9.2% and factitiously improve its angina outcomes. Exploiting such loopholes is more lucrative than improving efficiency or quality, giving creative cheaters a decisive market advantage.

78. The More Things Change Dept.: Death Rates Were Higher at For-Profit Hospitals in 1989

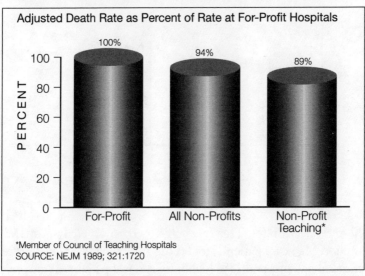

Adjusted Death Rate as Percent of Rate at For-Profit Hospitals

*Member of Council of Teaching Hospitals
SOURCE: NEJM 1989; 321:1720

Studies from the late 1990s have found higher death and complication rates at for-profit hospitals. But that news isn't new. More than a decade ago, a study (shown above) based on data for 3,100 hospitals found death rates 6% lower at non-profit community hospitals than at for-profits. Non-profit teaching hospitals' mortality rates were lower still; 11% below the for-profits'.

Other studies have found more post-operative complications and more preventable adverse events at for-profit hospitals than at private non-profits. Among the 60 top-ranked hospitals in the U.S.—shown to have lower death rates and better quality care—only one is investor-owned.

79. For-Profit Hospitals: Higher Mortality

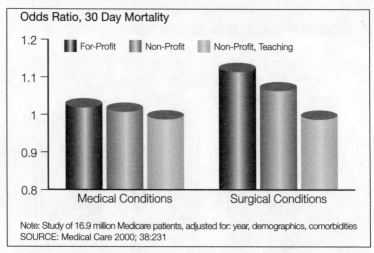

Odds Ratio, 30 Day Mortality

For-Profit   Non-Profit   Non-Profit, Teaching

Medical Conditions   Surgical Conditions

Note: Study of 16.9 million Medicare patients, adjusted for: year, demographics, comorbidities
SOURCE: Medical Care 2000; 38:231

Yet another recent study links for-profit ownership and high hospital death rates. This research, based on an analysis of 16.9 million Medicare patients, found the risk of dying 3% higher for medical patients and 13% higher for surgical patients at for-profit hospitals relative to non-profit teaching hospitals. The mortality rate at non-profit, non-teaching hospitals was intermediate.

80. More Nurses, Fewer Complications

A Study of 589 Hospitals in 10 States

- A one hour increase in RN hours/patient day was associated with:
    8.4% decrease in post-op pneumonia
    5.2% decrease in post-op thrombosis
    3.6% decrease in post-op pulmonary compromise
    8.9% decrease in post-op UTIs

- For-profit hospitals had higher rates of post-op pneumonia, pulmonary compromise & UTI, even after control for their lower RN staffing.

SOURCE: Kovner & Gergen—Image: J Nurs Schol 1998;30:315

Market pressures are pushing many hospitals to cut nurse staffing, and to substitute less-trained personnel for RNs. The study shown above found that hospitals with more RNs had lower rates of complications after surgery. A recent study of ICUs in the British journal *The Lancet* found that better RN staffing lowered death rates.

In the study of post-operative complications, investor-owned hospitals fared poorly on two accounts. They had lower RN staffing levels than non-profits. But even after taking into account their poor nurse staffing, investor-owned hospitals had higher than expected complication rates.

81. Nursing Home Staffing

Low Standards, Poor Working Conditions

- Required: 1 RN—8 hrs/day
               I LPN—24 hrs/day

- RNs + LPNs = only 30% of nursing staff

- Pay = 15–20% below hospitals

- Turnover rates = 80–100%/year

SOURCE: C. Harrington, UCSF—1997

The nursing home industry in the U.S. provides another illustration of the problems inherent in for-profit healthcare. Investor-owned facilities account for two-thirds of the U.S. nursing home industry, the shabbiest and lowest quality sector of our healthcare system. Professional staffing is scant, and staff are poorly paid—for perhaps the most difficult work in healthcare.

Several studies have found lower quality at for-profit nursing homes than at non-profits. For instance, for-profit homes receive more quality deficiency citations and have lower nurse staffing ratios.

82. Keep the Money Flowing

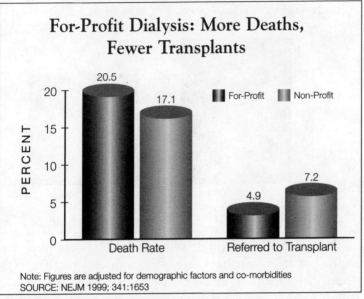

For-Profit Dialysis: More Deaths, Fewer Transplants

Note: Figures are adjusted for demographic factors and co-morbidities
SOURCE: NEJM 1999; 341:1653

Medicare pays for virtually all kidney dialysis under a special kidney disease program. Yet 85% of U.S. dialysis facilities are for-profit—dominated by a single German firm, Fresenius. Medicare pays a set fee per dialysis. The name of the game should be familiar: firms that skimp on care make larger profits. Death rates are 19.9% higher at for-profit dialysis facilities, even after statistical adjustment for patients' age, sex, race, and severity of illness.

Moreover, non-profit dialysis facilities are 47% more likely to refer their patients for transplants. When patients with renal (kidney) failure receive a kidney transplant, quality of life improves and they no longer require dialysis treatments. But a successful kidney transplant means lost business for the dialysis center.

83. For-Profit Dialysis for Children

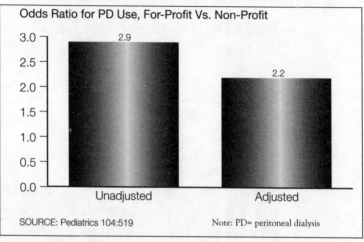

Odds Ratio for PD Use, For-Profit Vs. Non-Profit

SOURCE: Pediatrics 104:519   Note: PD= peritoneal dialysis

Peritoneal dialysis (PD), when possible, is the preferred method of treatment for kidney failure in children. For peritoneal dialysis, a small amount of clean fluid is infused into the patient's abdomen. Over a period of hours, urea and other toxins seep from the patient's blood into the fluid, which is then removed. This allows the blood to be cleansed of urea and other chemicals without the cumbersome machinery needed for hemodialysis (in which blood must be removed from the body for cleansing). While hemodialysis generally requires lengthy treatments at a dialysis clinic several times each week, peritoneal dialysis treatments can be done at home, minimizing the disruption of the child's life. Unfortunately, dialysis firms make larger profits from hemodialysis, and seldom offer peritoneal dialysis.

As shown above, children treated in non-profit facilities are about twice as likely to get the preferred (peritoneal) treatment, even after adjustment for confounding factors.

84. End Stage Kidney Disease Care

85% of U.S. providers are for-profit, outcomes are worse than Canada's

- U.S. death rates for dialysis patients are 47% higher after control for age, sex, race and comorbidities

- Canadians get more transplants (35% vs. 17%)

- 57% of U.S. patents are treated with reprocessed dialyzers, 0% in Canada

- Costs lower in Canada by $503/patient/month

- Fresenius (a German firm) controls 24% of U.S. market; profit = $225/patient/month

SOURCE: Med Care 1997; 35:686 & Fresenius SEC filings, 2000

The study shown above compared the outcomes of treatment for end-stage kidney disease (complete loss of kidney function) in the U.S. and Canada. Canadian patients fared better than comparable U.S. patients.

In the U.S., most dialysis clinics are for-profit. At the time of this study, the largest dialysis provider, National Medical Care (NMC—since taken over by the German firm, Fresenius) controlled 21% of the market. NMC manufactured dialyzers and labeled them "single use." However, at its own clinics NMC reused dialyzers, saving the firm about $130 million annually. NMC physicians shared in these profits. Fresenius currently cares for more than 60,000 Americans with kidney failure. In 2000, the firm paid a $486 million fine to settle charges of conspiring to defraud Medicare by charging for unnecessary tests and treatments, and violating anti-kickback laws by providing payments, yacht trips, and bear-hunting excursions in Alaska for potential customers.

For-profit dialysis centers are 55% more likely to use short dialysis (i.e., treat patients for fewer minutes per visit), which decreases survival but increases profits. Average dialysis hours per week are 10 in the U.S., compared to 12 in Germany and 14 in Japan. The difference in the death toll is stark: annual dialysis mortality is 23.6% in the U. S., 10% in Germany, and 9.7% in Japan.

85. The Jury is In

Investor-Owned Care

Summary of Evidence

- Hospitals: Costs 3%–11% higher, fewer nurses, higher overhead, death rates 6%–7% higher, fraud

- HMOs: Higher overhead, worse quality, collaboration with tobacco industry

- Dialysis: Death rates 20% higher, less use of transplants & peritoneal dialysis, fraud

- Nursing homes: More citations for poor quality, fraud

- Rehab Hospitals: Costs 19% higher

No evidence shows that for-profit HMOs, hospitals, or other facilities are more efficient than non-profits. Investor ownership is associated with higher costs in acute-care and rehabilitation hospitals. Costs in for-profit and non-profit HMOs and dialysis facilities are virtually identical. Quality of care is lower at for-profit hospitals, HMOs, dialysis clinics, and nursing homes.

Yet we object to investor-owned care because it wastes tax-payers' money and causes modest decrements in quality. More important, it embodies a new value system that severs the community roots and Samaritan traditions of hospitals, makes doctors and nurses into instruments of investors, and views patients as commodities.

In non-profit settings, greed vies with beneficence for the soul of medicine; investor-ownership marks the triumph of greed. In non-profits, a fiscal conundrum constrains altruism: "no money, no mission." In for-profits, form follows profit: the money is the mission.

CHAPTER 8

Thinking Clearly on Drugs

PHARMACEUTICAL PROFITEERING

Drug companies are the largest for-profit healthcare firms. In the past decade drug costs have soared (86). In the U.S., where firms have escaped the price regulations prevalent in other nations, drug prices are outrageous (87), fueling drug firm profits that outstrip any other industry (88). Meanwhile, pharmaceutical firms have wielded their political might to minimize their taxes (89). While the firms tout their high research (R & D) spending (much of it squandered on developing useless minor modifications of existing best-sellers), they spend far more on marketing and profits than on R&D (90). Marketing not only wastes money but also misleads physicians, worsens their prescribing (91), and distorts research (92).

86. An Expensive Habit

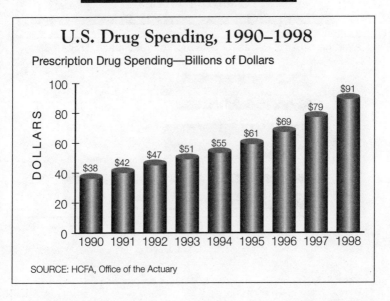

U.S. Drug Spending, 1990–1998

Prescription Drug Spending—Billions of Dollars

SOURCE: HCFA, Office of the Actuary

In recent years, drug costs have grown more rapidly than any other component of health spending. From an annual growth rate of 8.7% in 1993, drug spending accelerated to 15.4% annual growth in 1998. Prescription drugs accounted for 5.6% of total health spending in 1993, rising to 7.9% of spending in 1998. Drug costs consumed 6.6% of private insurance premiums in 1993, rising to 12.7% in 1998. For Medicaid, pharmaceuticals' share of spending rose from 6.4% to 9.1% over the same period.

As described in detail on subsequent pages, this increase has been driven by intensive marketing of new drugs, and pricing strategies that assure record profits for drug firms. Meanwhile, the rush to market new drugs has resulted in a record number of drugs being pulled off the market because of safety hazards overlooked in the approval process.

87. U.S. Seniors Pay More for Ten Top Selling Drugs*

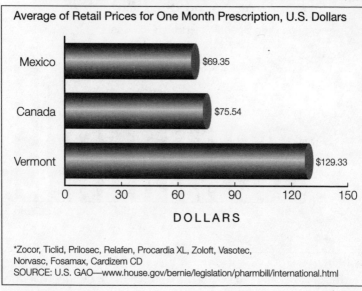

Average of Retail Prices for One Month Prescription, U.S. Dollars

Mexico — $69.35
Canada — $75.54
Vermont — $129.33

DOLLARS

*Zocor, Ticlid, Prilosec, Relafen, Procardia XL, Zoloft, Vasotec, Norvasc, Fosamax, Cardizem CD
SOURCE: U.S. GAO—www.house.gov/bernie/legislation/pharmbill/international.html

Prilosec, the world's best selling heartburn and ulcer medicine, costs $3.30 a pill in the U.S. and $1.47 in Canada. The allergy drug, Claritin, goes for $2 per pill in the U.S. but only 48 cents in Australia and 41 cents in Britain. A patient in Vermont pays $95 per month for Tamoxifen, a breast cancer medicine, but can get the same pills for $15 twenty miles away in Canada.

U.S. consumers have little bargaining power with the drug industry. While HMOs and other large purchasers like the Defense Department often negotiate steep discounts from drug makers, such discounts are unavailable to individual buyers. In other nations where government insurance programs cover more drug costs, government uses its clout to hold down prices.

As a result, Americans pay more for prescription drugs than people elsewhere.

Seniors are hard hit by high drug prices. One-third of seniors have no insurance for outpatient medications, and many forego vital medications. Among hypertensive seniors, those without drug coverage are 40% more likely to go without blood pressure medication. Seniors in poor health who lacked drug coverage were spending, on average, $750 out-of-pocket in 1996—a figure that's surely risen to above $1000 annually. Total drug spending per diabetic senior averaged $2278 in 1998, and more than 5% of seniors with chronic illnesses spent more than 5% of their incomes for medications.

Not surprisingly, drug firms oppose any policy that might hold down their prices. Thus, they've fought any proposal to expand Medicare coverage of outpatient medications which might allow Medicare to negotiate prices. For the same reason, they are staunch opponents of national health insurance (NHI); though NHI would expand their market, it would likely hold down prices and profits.

Cutting the cost of drugs is one area where the often maligned "government bureaucracy" can protect consumers. Drug price controls in most nations are managed by tiny government agencies that are part of larger national health systems. In Australia, a six person agency negotiates drug prices. In Canada, a board with a $2 million budget negotiates discounts that save Canadians $1.5 billion off U.S. prices annually. In the U.K., the government won a 4.5% price cut in 1999.

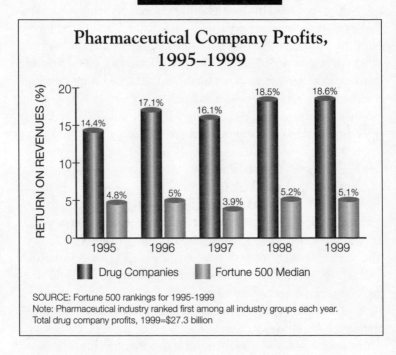

Pharmaceutical Company Profits, 1995–1999

RETURN ON REVENUES (%)

Year	Drug Companies	Fortune 500 Median
1995	14.4%	4.8%
1996	17.1%	5%
1997	16.1%	3.9%
1998	18.5%	5.2%
1999	18.6%	5.1%

■ Drug Companies   ■ Fortune 500 Median

SOURCE: Fortune 500 rankings for 1995-1999
Note: Pharmaceutical industry ranked first among all industry groups each year.
Total drug company profits, 1999=$27.3 billion

Drug companies have recorded the highest profits among all Fortune 500 industry groups for the past several years. In 1999, drug firms' profits totaled $27.3 billion. Merck's profits amounted to $5.9 billion; Johnson & Johnson made $4.2 billion; Pfizer, $3.2 billion; and Eli Lilly, $2.7 billion.

Pharmaceutical executives also pocket millions of dollars—and their incomes aren't counted as part of a company's profits. Pfizer's CEO made $15.2 million in 1999; Pharmacia's, $15.1 million; Schering-Plough's, $12.5 million; and Merck's, $6.1 million. And these figures don't reflect these executives' massive stock options.

89. Drug Firms Avoid Taxes

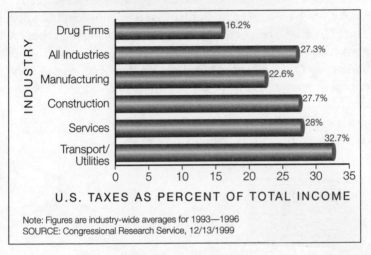

Note: Figures are industry-wide averages for 1993—1996
SOURCE: Congressional Research Service, 12/13/1999

Drug company lobbyists have won preferential treatment for the industry. Consequently, the pharmaceutical industry pays far lower-than-average taxes. In addition, taxpayers often fund research that discovers new compounds, which are later patented and marketed by private firms. There's nothing inherently wrong with taxpayers footing the bill for research—as long as we retain some ownership of the investment, and the right to use that research for the greater social good.

For instance, the NIH paid for most of the research to develop Xalatan, an important glaucoma drug. But Pharmacia & Upjohn later patented the drug, which brought in $507 million in 1999. The drug is actually made by a Hungarian chemical firm, which sells it in bulk to Pharmacia & Upjohn for $5 million annually—pennies per dose. Eventually, a patient pays $49.69 for a six-week supply at a pharmacy. Pharmacia spends about 40% of its revenue on marketing and administrative expenses, more than twice what it spends on research. In 1999, it expanded its sales force by 30% to 6,500 people.

Recent changes in Food and Drug Administration (FDA) regulations have also greatly enhanced drug firms' profitability. The FDA has lowered the standard for drug approval, relies on payments from the drug companies themselves for much of its budget, and now allows medical device manufacturers to contract with private firms for the legally-required device evaluations. As a result, new drugs are approved faster, but several dangerous drugs, such as the diabetes medication Troglitazone, have slipped through the approval process.

90. Where Prescription Dollars Go

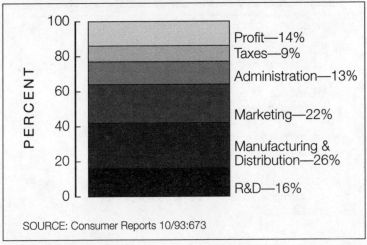

SOURCE: Consumer Reports 10/93:673

Drug companies claim that the high price of prescription drugs is necessary to support high research and development (R&D) costs. Yet R&D costs are dwarfed by marketing and profits, which together consume more than one-third of each prescription dollar. Moreover, the 13% spent on "administration" includes huge salaries for drug company executives, plush offices, and huge lobbying operations.

No audited figures are available on the amount drug companies spend for advertising. The Office for Technology Assessment estimated that total marketing costs would consume 22% of prescription drug spending, about $27 billion in 2000. Industry consultants estimate 1998 drug promotion costs at $8.3 billion, including $1.3 billion for direct-to-consumer advertising, up 55% from 1997. The 10 drugs most heavily promoted in these ads accounted for 20% of the total increase in drug spending last year.

91. Confusing the Doctors: Drug Company Sponsored Miseducation

- Spending for drug promotion (>$10 billion/yr.) exceeds total medical student teaching costs

- The average MD meets with one of the 56,000 drug reps once a week

- Attending drug company-sponsored CME predicts worse prescribing

- 11% of drug reps' factual claims are false (all favorable)—26% of MDs recognize even one falsehood

SOURCE: JAMA 283:373 & 273:1296, Ann Int Med 116:919, and www.nofreelunch.org

Drug company promotion costs not only add to the price of drugs, but reduce the quality of care. In 1998, drug firms employed 56,000 sales representatives (up from 35,000 in 1994) who made 59 million visits (so-called "details") to physicians. That's nearly 1 drug rep for every 11 practicing physicians. In 1998, Pfizer made 1.226 million details for Trovan (a new antibiotic later found to cause liver failure) making it the most promoted drug in the U.S. that year. After record sales in its first 12 months, the FDA sharply limited use of the drug because of reports of severe liver toxicity. Monsanto expects to make 2.5 million visits in 2000 to push Celebrex, a new arthritis drug.

Interns and residents receive, on average, 6 gifts per year from drug firms; most residents believe that gifts have no influence on their behavior (no data on gifts are available for other physicians). Most doctors believe that drug reps provide accurate information about their drugs, despite also believing that reps prioritize drug promotion above patient welfare and are likely to use unethical practices. Physicians who meet with drug reps—or accept meals, honoraria, or travel funds from them—are more likely to request that the promoted drugs be added to a hospital's formulary; most of the drugs added to formularies in this way offer no therapeutic advantage.

Exposure to drug rep speakers at conferences is associated with learning and disseminating inaccurate information, and with inappropriate prescribing. In drug-company sponsored continuing medical education programs, the sponsor's drug is virtually always preferentially highlighted, and attendees change prescribing practices in favor of the sponsor's drug.

While some HMOs have used formularies (approved lists of drugs) to control physicians' prescribing practices, the HMO formularies can create new problems. HMOs make frequent changes in the formularies, usually for economic rather than clinical reasons. This forces doctors to constantly switch patients from one drug to another, increasing the likelihood of dosing errors, allergic reactions, and other medication problems.

92. Commercialized Science

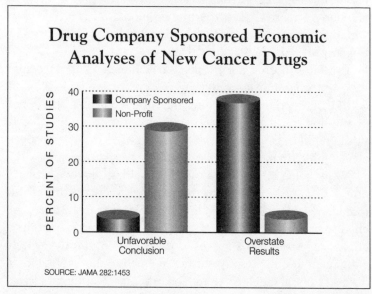

Drug Company Sponsored Economic Analyses of New Cancer Drugs

SOURCE: JAMA 282:1453

Many studies document the biased nature of drug-company sponsored research reports, journal articles, conferences, advertising claims, and "expert" opinion. Yet drug firms play an increasing role in sponsoring research and education. At present, most U.S. psychiatric research is funded by drug firms. Small wonder that psychiatric research focuses on expensive drug treatments, often minimizing drug side effects and overestimating long-term positive effects.

CHAPTER 9

Solutions are at Hand

OTHER NATIONS DO BETTER

The problems detailed in the previous chapters are doubly tragic because solutions have long been available. International experience proves that universal coverage is feasible and improves health. Every other developed nation assures health coverage for the entire population (93). Our infant mortality rate, among the lowest in the world in 1950, is now disturbingly high (94). We trail other nations on life expectancy for both women (95) and men (96), and score poorly on measures of premature death (97). Meanwhile, our health costs per capita are nearly double those of any other nation, and rising more rapidly (98). Indeed, GOVERNMENT spending on healthcare in the U.S. exceeds TOTAL health spending per capita in any other nation (99). Government spending includes not only Medicare and Medicaid, but also public expenditures to purchase private insurance for government workers and tax subsidies for private insurance (100). These massive tax subsidies are sharply regressive, offering little to a poor family and thousands of dollars to a wealthy one (101).

Our high medical costs cannot be blamed on the elderly; other nations have older populations (102). Nor are Americans voracious consumers of care. We have fewer physician visits (103) and lower hospital use per capita (104) than other nations. Surveys of English-speaking countries show that Americans face the greatest barriers to obtaining care (105). Moreover, our managed-care-dominated system frequently forces people to switch doctors, disrupting the continuity of care (106).

93. The U.S. Stands Alone

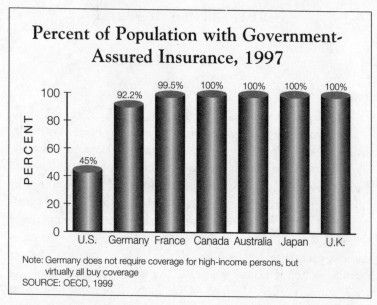

Percent of Population with Government-Assured Insurance, 1997

Note: Germany does not require coverage for high-income persons, but virtually all buy coverage
SOURCE: OECD, 1999

The U.S. is the only developed nation without universal health coverage. Note that while virtually all Germans are covered by health insurance, about 8% choose private insurance rather than enrolling in one of the quasi-public insurance funds.

94. A Small Matter of Life and Death

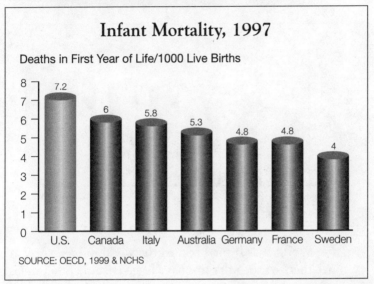

Infant Mortality, 1997

Deaths in First Year of Life/1000 Live Births

SOURCE: OECD, 1999 & NCHS

Despite spending far more on medical care than any other nation, the U.S. continues to fall behind in measures of health.

While the infant mortality rate in the U.S. has fallen, it has done so more slowly than infant mortality rates in other developed nations. In 1960 the U.S. ranked 12th among 29 industrialized nations, falling to 21st in 1990 and 24th in 1997.

95. No Longer First: Life Expectancy for Women, 1997

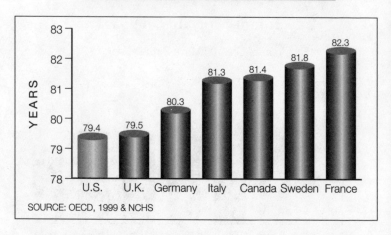

SOURCE: OECD, 1999 & NCHS

After World War II the U.S. led the world in life expectancy. Since then, our health gains have lagged behind other industrialized nations'. In 1960, the United States ranked 13th of 29 developed nations in life expectancy for women. By 1990 the U.S. ranking had slipped to 17th, and by 1997 to 20th.

96. Life Expectancy for Men, 1997

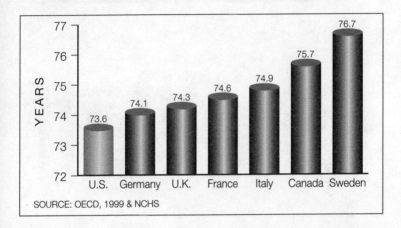

SOURCE: OECD, 1999 & NCHS

As with the women, so go the men: Life expectancy has risen very slowly in the U.S. in recent years, causing us to lag behind other developed nations. For men, the U.S. ranked 17th for life expectancy in 1960, falling to 21st in 1990 and 22nd 1997.

97. We Are the Biggest Losers: Potential Years of Life Lost per 100,000

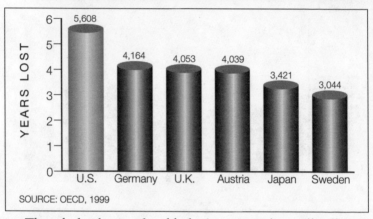

SOURCE: OECD, 1999

Though death rates for elderly Americans (virtually all covered by Medicare) are similar to death rates of the elderly in other developed nations, death rates for American children and young adults are dramatically higher than those of other developed nations.

Potential Years of Life Lost (PYLL) is a summary measure of premature deaths. It gives greater weight to deaths occurring at younger ages, which are more likely to be preventable. The calculation of PYLL involves adding up deaths occurring at each age and multiplying this by the number of remaining years to live until the age of 70.

98. U.S. Costs Rose More Rapidly Than Other Nations'

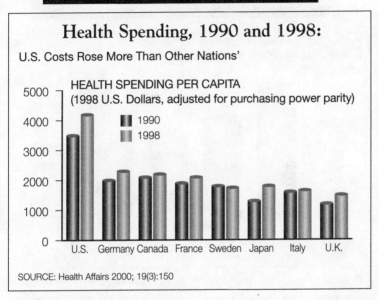

Health Spending, 1990 and 1998:

U.S. Costs Rose More Than Other Nations'

HEALTH SPENDING PER CAPITA
(1998 U.S. Dollars, adjusted for purchasing power parity)

■ 1990
▨ 1998

SOURCE: Health Affairs 2000; 19(3):150

The slowdown in the rise in U.S. healthcare costs in the early 1990s received wide media coverage and has been cited by supporters of the healthcare status quo as proof that reform is not needed. Yet our health costs continue to be higher than other nations', and have risen more in recent years. By 1998, the U.S. was spending $4,270 per capita, about twice the spending of Germany ($2,400), Canada ($2,250), France ($2,120), Sweden ($1,820) or Japan ($1,780). Italy spent $1660 per capita and the U.K. $1450. Switzerland (data not shown on graph) had the world's second most expensive healthcare, $2,740 per capita.

Between 1990 and 1998, U.S. health spending (adjusted for inflation) increased 22%. Of the nations shown above, only Japan had a higher rate of increase. Per capita costs actually fell in Sweden, and were stable in Italy and Canada.

99. U.S. Public Spending Per Capita for Health is Greater than Total Spending in Other Nations

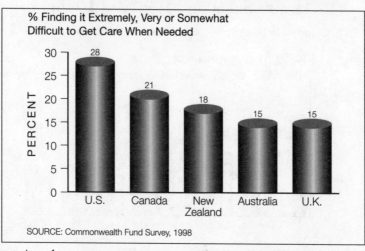

% Finding it Extremely, Very or Somewhat Difficult to Get Care When Needed

SOURCE: Commonwealth Fund Survey, 1998

Another argument against a single payer healthcare system is that Americans would never tolerate such a large role for the government. But government plays a much larger role in financing healthcare in the U.S. than is commonly acknowledged. In fact, government health spending in the U.S.—$2,544 per capita in 1997—exceeded total health spending in any other nation except Switzerland. Government spending includes Medicare, Medicaid, Veterans Administration programs, as well as insurance premiums for government employees and tax subsidies for private insurance. Americans already pay enough for government-paid healthcare to fully fund a national health insurance system more generous than Canada's. Then we pay an additional $1,551 per capita out-of-pocket and to private insurers.

100. For Whom the Bill Tolls: Who Pays for Healthcare?

	Amount in 1998 (Billions)	Percent
Government	$736.8	64.1%
Medicare	$216.2	
Medicaid	$170.6	
Premiums for public employees	$67.3	
Tax subsidy for private insurance	$124.8	
Other*	$157.9	
Private Employers	$216.5	18.8%
Individuals (excludes tax subsidy)	$195.8	17.0%
TOTAL	**$1149.1**	**100%**

*Includes VA, NIH, subsidy for public hospitals, worker's comp, health departments, etc.
SOURCE: Himmelstein & Woolhandler—Unpublished analysis of NCHS data, Health Affairs 1999; 18(2):176

Single payer national health insurance would eliminate employers' role in healthcare, leading some policy wonks to question the feasibility of such reform. But federal, state, and local governments currently pay nearly two-thirds of health costs, and government's share of spending has been gradually increasing in recent years.

Private employers' role in paying for healthcare is smaller than commonly believed—accounting for less than one-fifth of total spending—and hardly justifies their decisive influence over health policy. Though "employer-sponsored" private health insurance covers about 60% of Americans, this widely cited figure overstates the private employers' role. First, it includes over 20 million government employees (e.g., teachers, police, firefighters) and their dependents whose private coverage is funded through our taxes. Second, it includes workers who purchased their coverage through an employer-sponsored plan, but whose employer made no financial contribution towards the coverage. Finally, it includes a large number of individuals with employer-paid supplemental coverage (Medigap), but whose primary insurer is Medicare. Hence, only about 40% of Americans have their primary health insurance coverage paid wholly or in part by a private employer.

Both Republicans and some Democrats have advocated market-driven health policies i.e., turning over most of Medicare and Medicaid to private HMOs, and encouraging for-profit care. Yet it is an odd free market that relies so heavily on public dollars. In effect, U.S. healthcare is publicly funded but privately controlled.

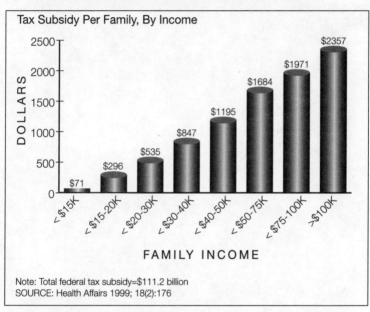

Tax Subsidy Per Family, By Income

Note: Total federal tax subsidy=$111.2 billion
SOURCE: Health Affairs 1999; 18(2):176

Health insurance premiums are largely tax-exempt when provided through an employer. The employer's share is not taxed as income to the employee (and is tax deductible as a business expense for the employer). The employee's share may also be tax-exempt in firms with "flexible spending plans." Since tax rates are higher for higher income employees, the value of these tax exemptions rises with income, as shown above.

In 1998, the Federal tax subsidy for private health benefits totaled $111.2 billion (more than the Federal Government's share of Medicaid); state subsidies added $13.6 billion. Though families making more than $100,000 per year account for only 10% of the population, they receive 23.6% of the tax subsidy.

68.7% of the tax subsidy went to families with incomes of $50,000 or more (36% of the population). Less than one-third of the tax subsidy for healthcare went to the 64% of the population with incomes below $50,000.

While politicians often focus on reining in government spending for the poor, they rarely mention the massive tax subsidies for the wealthy.

102. Are We Too Old or Too Ill to Afford Universal Healthcare?

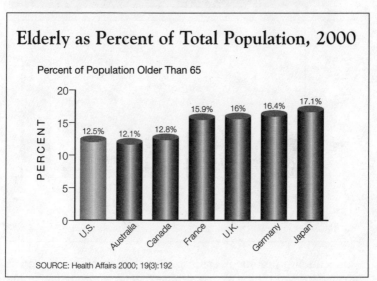

Elderly as Percent of Total Population, 2000

Percent of Population Older Than 65

SOURCE: Health Affairs 2000; 19(3):192

Some argue that our healthcare problems are the result of bad habits or skewed demographics and hence can't be blamed on the private system. Policy analysts frequently cite the burgeoning elderly population as a major cause of rising healthcare costs. Yet many nations with far lower healthcare costs (and universal coverage) have a higher proportion of elders.

Another policy canard blames extraordinary care of the dying for rising costs. Yet Medicare expenditure for care in the last year of life has remained constant at about 28% of Medicare spending for two decades.

Nor can high U.S. healthcare costs be attributed to HIV, drug abuse, or violence. HIV costs account for about 1.5% of U.S. health spending. Alcohol and tobacco use dwarf elicit drugs as causes of death, disease, and health spending—and other nations suffer even higher rates of alcoholism and tobacco addiction.

103. Do Americans Want Too Much? Physician Visits per Capita

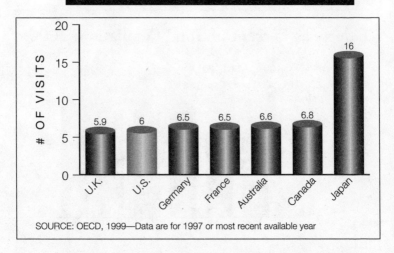

SOURCE: OECD, 1999—Data are for 1997 or most recent available year

A standard argument against a single payer health plan is that Americans use more healthcare than such a plan could provide. But aside from a few people afflicted by hypochondriasis, Americans are not insatiable consumers of medical care. We visit physicians less often than people in most other nations. High utilization of care cannot explain our high medical costs relative to other nations.

104. Hospital Inpatient Days Per Capita

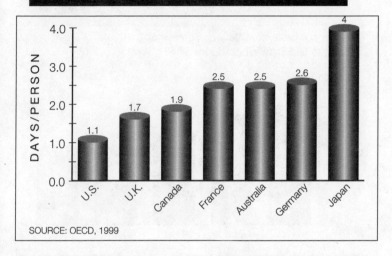

SOURCE: OECD, 1999

Many U.S. health policy leaders blame rising health costs on the American people for using too much care. In this view, cost containment must curtail services through co-payments, managed-care bureaucracies, and incentives for physicians to withhold care. However, Americans get less of most types of health services than people in nations with much lower health expenditures. Indeed, the U.S. has among the shortest average lengths of hospital stay, yet by far the highest hospital cost in the world.

Even for many high technology procedures—e.g., kidney, heart, lung, and bone marrow transplants—U.S. rates are no higher than those of several other nations. Japan has more MRI scanners per capita, but far lower healthcare costs.

105. U.S. Trails in Access: Difficulties Getting Needed Care

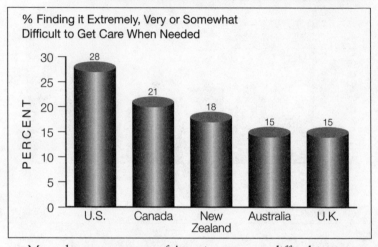

% Finding it Extremely, Very or Somewhat Difficult to Get Care When Needed

PERCENT

U.S.	Canada	New Zealand	Australia	U.K.
28	21	18	15	15

More than one quarter of Americans report difficulties in getting needed care, including half a million people who are turned away from emergency rooms each year because they cannot pay.

Many of those with access problems have coverage. Of the 49 million people who reported problems paying medical bills over a one year period, 28 million had private coverage; 4 million had Medicare; 5 million had Medicaid; and only 12 million were uninsured. In 1997, 6% of those covered by insurance throughout the year reported not filling a prescription because of cost; 7% reported not getting needed care. Among those who had coverage for only part of the year, 21% failed to fill a prescription and 21% failed to get needed care.

Residents of other nations report many fewer access problems, as shown above. In addition, Americans are twice as likely as Canadians or Britons to fail to fill a prescription because of costs; and three or more times as likely to spend more than $750 out-of-pocket for healthcare or have problems paying medical bills.

106. Continuity of Care: The U.S. Specializes in Cutting Patients Off From Their Doctors...

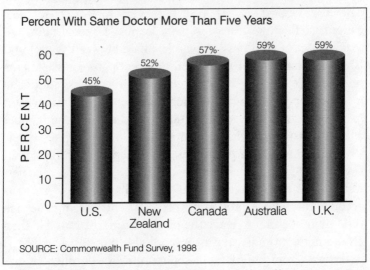

Percent With Same Doctor More Than Five Years

SOURCE: Commonwealth Fund Survey, 1998

The single payer systems of other nations allow patients to see virtually any doctor; insurers do not dictate provider choice. In contrast, restrictive health insurance plans in the U.S. often disrupt the continuity of care. Nearly one fifth of privately insured Americans change plans each year, often because of job loss, job change, because their employer changed plans, or because the plan has pulled out of their area in search of higher profits elsewhere. Twenty percent of Medicare HMO enrollees drop out within 12 months of joining. In Medicaid HMOs, about 5% of patients disenroll each month, usually because they've lost eligibility. Ephemeral medical relationships are becoming the norm. Patients are forced to change doctors whenever their employer changes health plans, because each plan has its own restricted list of providers. Indeed, the very theory of market competition demands willingness to switch health plans in search of the best deal.

These disruptions exact a price, both clinically and economically. Studies have shown that patients remaining with the same doctor incur lower costs, especially for hospital care. The cost curve appears "S" shaped, with very high costs for new patients (reflecting, at least in part, people who sought out care at the onset of an illness), a plateau phase between years 1 and 10, and a further fall thereafter. Giving doctors and patients time to get to know each other enables clinical parsimony. The intimacy and continuity of doctor/patient interactions also improves compliance with treatment, and reduces the number of hypertensive patients lost to follow-up.

Continuity of care probably saves society money. But for an HMO, the costs of long-term patient/doctor relationships outweigh the modest savings. Since a small number of patients account for a large proportion of costs, encouraging the sick (and their doctors) to leave the plan is far more profitable than promoting continuity. Business sense also dictates that HMOs walk away from unprofitable communities or enrollee groups. Firing (delisting) experienced doctors may make good business sense; doctors tend to accumulate older, sicker, and more expensive-to-treat patients over time. The threat of being fired may intimidate doctors into toeing the managed-care line.

CHAPTER 10

Northern Light

CANADA'S EXPERIENCE WITH NATIONAL HEALTH INSURANCE

As the U.S. was implementing Medicare and Medicaid in the mid-1960s, Canada was putting in place national health insurance. The Canadian Government offered the provinces substantial funding for universal, comprehensive, publicly administered coverage (107). Within one year of the program's start-up, the proportion of patients with serious symptoms who saw a doctor increased sharply (108). Infant mortality—which had long been higher than in the U.S.—fell rapidly, and has remained below the U.S. level (109). While universal healthcare has not erased inequalities in health, it has ameliorated them. Even poor infants in Canada have death rates below the U.S. average (110). While homeless men in Toronto have higher death rates than the non-homeless, they fare far better than homeless men in U.S. cities (111).

Despite waits for some specialized care, peer-reviewed studies continue to find that quality of care for the average Canadian is at least as good as the care received by INSURED Americans (though Canada spends far less). Depressed Canadians receive more professional help, and more appropriate treatment than their American counterparts (112). Canada has lower surgical death rates than the U.S., and lower cancer death rates for potentially curable tumors. Waits for cataract surgery are decreasing, though surgeons who have private practices (and can presumably increase their private referrals by maximizing waits in the public system) appear to inflate the waiting times (113).

Seniors in Canada actually get more of most types of physician care than American seniors (114). Meanwhile, medicine has remained a highly respected and desirable career in Canada, attracting twice as many applicants per medical school place as in the U.S. (115). In sum, despite spending roughly half what we do, Canadians enjoy better health, the security of universal coverage, and a system that is relatively free of bureaucracy and constraints on patient choice (116).

Yet Canada also has problems (117). Wealthy Canadians, whose taxes help subsidize the coverage of the less affluent (118), have pushed conservative governments to cut health spending—particularly hospital budgets. (In contrast, in the U.S. healthcare financing is highly regressive; the rich pay less (119)). In addition, as care has shifted from hospitals to home, and medication costs have risen, Canada's insurance has not kept pace; coverage of home care and outpatient drugs is patchy. These problems are amplified by U.S. and Canadian business groups anxious to undermine the public system and increase pressure for the expansion of private, for-profit medicine (120). In addition to media campaigns and lobbying in Canada, these firms have used the World Trade Organization to press their case against publicly-funded, non-profit healthcare (121).

National health insurance has effectively contained costs in Canada—perhaps too effectively (122). Canada's healthcare costs have been flat since the mid-1990s. Canada's single payer system greatly simplifies administration, cutting insurance overhead to about 1% (vs. 15% of premiums in the U.S.) and reducing bureaucratic costs for hospitals (123) and doctors (124). Overall, Canada saves about $857 per capita annually on bureaucracy alone (125). Additionally, Canada saves through improved health planning (e.g., minimizing the duplication of expensive services) and an emphasis on primary care.

107. Single-Payer Defined: Minimum Standards for Canada's Provincial Programs

1. Universal coverage that does not impede, either directly or indirectly, whether by charges or otherwise, reasonable access

2. Portability of benefits from province to province

3. Coverage for all medically necessary services

4. Publicly administered, non-profit program

Canada implemented national health insurance nationwide at about the same time that the U.S. implemented Medicare. Canada's program is run by the Provinces, with Federal financial assistance.

Each Provincial program must meet four criteria. 1) It must enroll virtually everyone in the Province and eliminate all out-of-pocket costs for covered services. 2) Benefits must be portable from Province to Province—if you are from Ontario and get sick in Quebec you must be covered. 3) The Provincial program must cover all medically-necessary services. The Federal government has not defined this requirement further, but all of the Provincial programs have enacted comprehensive coverage of hospital and physician care. Provinces vary in their coverage of dental services, eyeglasses, prescription drugs, and long-term care. The rising costs and inconsistent coverage of drugs and home care have emerged as problems in recent years. 4) The program must be administered through a public, non-profit agency. This requirement is based on strong evidence that public administration is far cheaper and more efficient that private insurance administration.

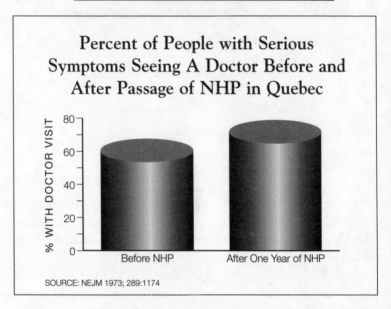

Percent of People with Serious Symptoms Seeing A Doctor Before and After Passage of NHP in Quebec

SOURCE: NEJM 1973; 289:1174

When Canada's National Health Program (NHP) was first implemented, researchers in Quebec studied the effects. Within one year, the proportion of residents with serious symptoms (e.g., chest pain, persistent cough, or vomiting blood) who actually saw a physician increased substantially. At the same time, waiting times for a routine appointment for wealthy Quebecers increased modestly. Overall, care shifted from the healthy towards the sick. The total number of physician visits in Quebec did not change. Physicians worked about the same number of hours before and after the insurance program came into effect; predictions of exploding usage by consumers, and sharply rising costs once care became free failed to materialize.

109. Canada Improving Faster

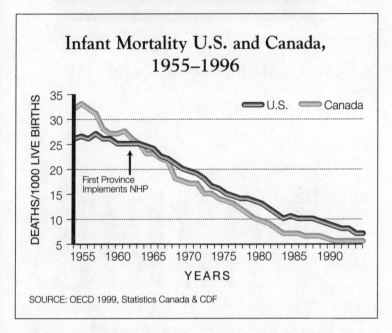

Infant Mortality U.S. and Canada, 1955–1996

DEATHS/1000 LIVE BIRTHS

U.S.　Canada

First Province
Implements NHP

YEARS

SOURCE: OECD 1999, Statistics Canada & CDF

Before the implementation of universal coverage, Canada's infant mortality rate was higher than the U.S.'s. Soon after, the Canadian infant death rate dipped below that of the U.S., and has remained lower.

National health insurance in Canada removed financial barriers to prenatal, obstetrical, and infant care. Financial problems remain the main reason why American women delay the prenatal care that could prevent many infant deaths.

Infant Deaths by Income, Canada 1996

Even the Poor Do Better Than U.S. Average

INFANT MORTALITY RATE

Wealthiest 20%	Next 20%	Middle 20%	Next 20%	Poorest 20%	U.S. Average
3.9	4.7	5.1	5.2	6.5	7.8

INCOME QUINTILES, CANADA

SOURCE: Health Reports 199; 11(3):25

While inequalities in health persist in Canada, they are far smaller than in the U.S. Even the poorest Canadians now have infant mortality rates below the U.S. average.

Poor Canadians enjoy equal access, even to expensive services that are in relatively short supply. Queues for coronary artery bypass surgery (CABS) in Canada have been widely publicized (and exaggerated) in the U.S. media. Yet poor Canadians have slightly higher rates of CABS than wealthy Canadians, a clinically appropriate pattern since heart disease is more common among the poor. In contrast, in New York State, the poor receive only half as many CABS as the wealthy (and fewer than the poor in Canada). Indeed, for virtually every medical problem that has been studied, the poor, the uninsured, and minority group members in the U.S. receive inappropriately low rates of care.

In a single payer health system that has no private component, money spent on health is for everyone regardless of ability to pay, and access is determined by need, not wealth.

111. Canada's Social Problems

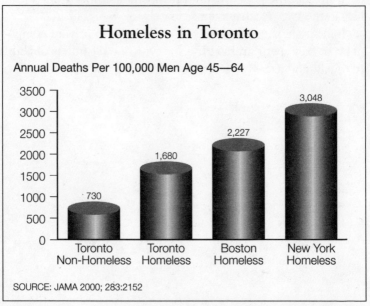

Homeless in Toronto

Annual Deaths Per 100,000 Men Age 45—64

730	1,680	2,227	3,048
Toronto Non-Homeless	Toronto Homeless	Boston Homeless	New York Homeless

SOURCE: JAMA 2000; 283:2152

Contrary to American stereotypes, Canada is an increasingly diverse society. Immigrants make up a larger fraction of the population in Canada than in the U.S. Moreover, Canada is not without social problems. Alcoholism is more prevalent than in the U.S., and Canadian cities have substantial numbers of homeless people. The homeless in Toronto have death rates more than twice Toronto's housed population. Yet universal access to healthcare appears to partially ameliorate the medical problems of Toronto's homeless, whose death rates are well below those of America's homeless.

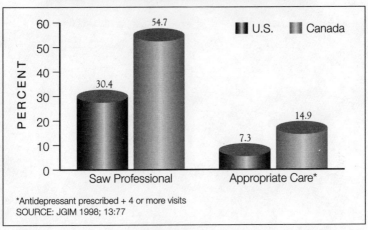

PERCENT

60
50
40
30
20
10
0

■ U.S.   ■ Canada

30.4

54.7

7.3

14.9

Saw Professional   Appropriate Care*

*Antidepressant prescribed + 4 or more visits
SOURCE: JGIM 1998; 13:77

Canadians with clinical depression are more likely than depressed Americans to receive professional help, and to receive appropriate care—medication plus ongoing care.

A pair of surveys in the U.S. and Canada (Ontario) used identical assessments of mental health needs and services. People in the U.S. were more likely than Canadians to report psychiatric disorders, poor mental health, or lost work time due to psychiatric problems. More Americans than Canadians had used outpatient mental health services within the past 12 months (13.3% vs. 8%). But all of the higher U.S. utilization was accounted for by people with no psychiatric disorder, or with milder psychiatric illness. Among those with serious mental illness, Canadians got more care. For instance, among people with 2 or more mental health diagnoses (as defined in the standard DSM guide), 24% of Canadians had seen a physician and 23% had seen a mental health specialist within the past year; of Americans, only 10% had seen a physician and 19%

had seen a mental health specialist. In contrast, 2.6% of Americans with no psychiatric disorder had seen a mental health specialist within the previous 12 months, vs. 1.2% of Canadians. Services are better targeted to need in Canada.

113. The Truth and Myth of Waiting Lines in Canada

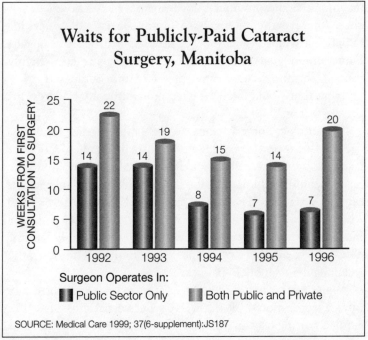

Waits for Publicly-Paid Cataract Surgery, Manitoba

WEEKS FROM FIRST CONSULTATION TO SURGERY

	1992	1993	1994	1995	1996
Public Sector Only	14	14	8	7	7
Both Public and Private	22	19	15	14	20

Surgeon Operates In:
■ Public Sector Only   ■ Both Public and Private

SOURCE: Medical Care 1999; 37(6-supplement):JS187

Queues for coronary surgery and other procedures have caused consternation in Canada, and have been publicized by U.S. insurance and drug firms opposed to national health insurance. Any discussion of waiting lists in Canada should start from the fact that Canada spends half as much per capita on healthcare as the U.S. Even modest spending increases in Canada would quickly erase virtually all queues.

For most kinds of care, waits are minimal in Canada—no longer than in the U.S. Doctors and hospitals provide emergency and urgent care without queuing. For non-urgent care, systematic surveys show that queues have not grown in recent years—though they have received wider publicity.

A variety of factors cause queuing. For radiotherapy, the problem is a shortage of technicians, not of expensive machines. Some provincial governments have chosen to purchase (and pay the bill for) a few highly specialized services like radiation therapy at nearby U.S. hospitals with excess capacity. Some remote areas of Canada have difficulty attracting highly-trained personnel, who often prefer cosmopolitan settings (a problem that would likely be even more difficult to address in a private system).

For cataract surgery, waits are generally modest, and have declined in recent years. However, a small number of eye surgeons who operate in both public hospitals and private clinics have accumulated long waiting lists for public hospital patients. Similar situations have arisen in the U.K. and New Zealand, where physicians can augment their private referrals and incomes by making care less available in the public setting. Thus, the availability of private care often undermines rather than augments publicly-paid care.

Waits for cardiac surgery have received the most attention (and exaggeration). Of 8,517 consecutive patients placed on cardiac waiting lists in Ontario, 3.2% of patients either declined surgery, or had surgery deferred on the advice of a cardiologist or surgeon. 0.4% of patients died while waiting for surgery and 3 people had surgery deferred after a non-fatal heart attack. Among the 8,213 patients who received surgery, the median wait was 17 days. The median wait for urgent cases was 1 day. Older patients waited no longer than younger patients. Waits varied considerably from hospital to hospital. At 2 hospitals, waits averaged 8 days, while at 1 hospital waits averaged 48 days. The clinical urgency of surgery was the best predictor of how long the patient waited.

114. Physician Services for the Elderly

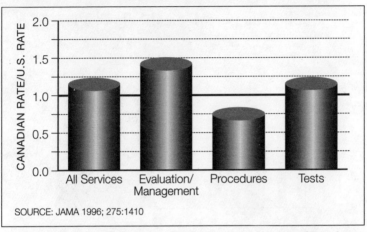

SOURCE: JAMA 1996; 275:1410

No credible study has found worse outcomes or quality of care for Canadians than for insured Americans. Though virtually all U.S. seniors have insurance (through Medicare) they actually receive less of most types of care than Canadian seniors.

Among elderly patients undergoing surgery, survival is better in Manitoba than in New England for 8 of the 10 procedures that have been studied. U.S. patients suffering heart attacks are more likely than Canadians to undergo invasive diagnostic procedures and surgery, but their rates of death or recurrent heart attack are identical. The overall death rate from heart disease is lower in Canada. Cancer case death rates are lower in Canada than in the U.S., especially for treatable cancers among low income and younger people. Relative to U.S. cities, Canadian cities have lower rates of hospitalizations that should be preventable through good ambulatory care. For instance, most hospitalizations for asthma should be preventable if patients have good primary care, affordable medications, and good access to telephone advice when their asthma first starts to flare up. Moreover, differences in preventable hospitalizations by social class are much smaller in Canada than in the U.S.

115. Pride in the Profession

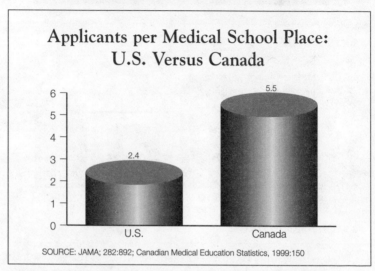

Applicants per Medical School Place: U.S. Versus Canada

- U.S.: 2.4
- Canada: 5.5

SOURCE: JAMA; 282:892; Canadian Medical Education Statistics, 1999:150

During the 1980s the number of applicants to U.S. medical schools plummeted, then rose slightly during the 1990s. Canada experienced no such decline. Medicine has remained a popular and respected profession in Canada. Polls indicate that Canadian physicians believe that national health insurance has improved the population's health, and prefer practice under national health insurance—though most are convinced that the system is now underfunded. In contrast, physician dissatisfaction has increased dramatically in the U.S. over the past 20 years.

One reason that Canadian medical schools get more applicants is their low tuition. The Canadian government has recognized that medical education is an integral part of medical care. It has chosen to subsidize medical schools "up-front" and keep tuition low rather than bearing the costs retrospectively through the higher physicians' incomes required to pay back medical school loans.

116. What's OK in Canada?

Compared to the U.S.

- Life expectancy two years longer

- Infant deaths 25% lower

- Universal comprehensive coverage

- More MD visits, hospital care; less bureaucracy

- Quality of care equivalent to insured Americans'

- Free choice of doctor/hospital

Canada's provincial single payer health insurance plans provide universal coverage and are far more efficient than U.S. healthcare. Despite spending about one half as much per capita as Americans, Canadians receive more of most types of care. They live longer, enjoy an unfettered choice of doctors and hospitals, and a quality of care that is on a par with the care of insured Americans. Finally, Canadians are secure that their healthcare will be covered.

117. What's the Matter in Canada?

- The wealthy lobby for private funding and tax cuts; they resent subsidizing care for others

- Result: Government funding cuts (e.g. 30% of hospital beds closed during 90s) causing dissatisfaction

- U.S. and Canadian firms seek profit opportunities in health care privatization

- Conrad Black, foe of public services, owns 2/3 of Canadian newspapers

- Misleading waiting list surveys by right wing group

Ten years ago, Canadians were more satisfied with their healthcare system than any other nation. Over the past decade the Canadian government has decreased funding for national health insurance, causing painful cuts in care (especially in hospitals), and shifting some costs onto individuals. Meanwhile, costs for medications and home care, which are not covered under the single payer plan in most provinces, have risen. As a result, dissatisfaction has increased. Right-wing politicians have played upon this discontent (a result of the cuts they themselves implemented) to rally support for privatization. Nonetheless, Canadians still show greater confidence in their system than Americans, and have recently forced politicians to commit additional funds to care.

Wealthy Canadians supported the funding cuts of the 1990s as a means to reduce income/resource transfer from themselves to the poor. Cutting public funding (and taxes) and allowing private insurance to fill the gaps, allows the wealthy to improve their own coverage without subsidizing better coverage for those with lower incomes. Healthcare firms also lobbied for privatization to open new profit opportunities. Insurers sought to sell more policies, and hospitals and other providers sought freedom from the profit-limiting regulations of government payers.

Throughout the 1990s, conservative ideologues attacked healthcare. The Fraser Institute (a business-funded group in Canada that has also advocated privatizing whales and abolishing the licensure of physicians) produced shoddy studies purporting to document huge waiting lists for care—studies controverted by more careful analyses. Right-wing media, particularly the two-thirds of Canadian daily newspapers owned by Conrad Black, widely publicized the Fraser studies.

118. Who Pays for Canada's NHP?

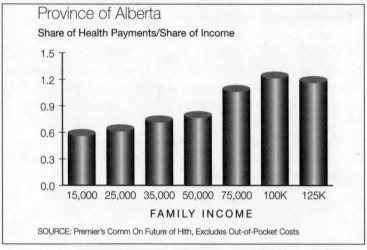

Province of Alberta

Share of Health Payments/Share of Income

FAMILY INCOME

SOURCE: Premier's Comm On Future of Hlth, Excludes Out-of-Pocket Costs

Because Canada's National Healthcare Program (NHP) is largely tax-funded, and the tax system takes a larger share of income from wealthy individuals than from the poor, the financing of Canada's system is progressive. The wealthy pay a higher share of their incomes, while the poor pay less.

Moreover, Canada's system assures a larger subsidy from the healthy to the sick by minimizing co-payments and out-of-pocket costs which sick (but not healthy) patients must bear. In Canada, the sick pay no more for their insurance coverage than the healthy, and out-of-pocket costs are low. In contrast, in the U.S., insurance premiums for the sick are often sky high, and serious illness brings huge out-of-pocket bills, even for those with coverage. Sickness can create financial hardship in any system, especially when it throws a person out of work. The sick are sometimes in the worst position to pay for care. A compassionate system spreads the financial burden of caring for society's ill broadly across the population.

119. Who Pays for Healthcare?
The Regressivity of U.S. Health Financing

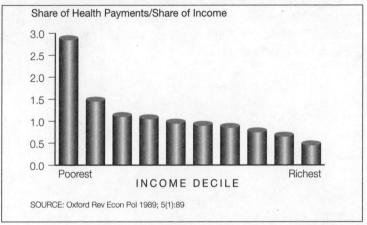

Share of Health Payments/Share of Income

INCOME DECILE

SOURCE: Oxford Rev Econ Pol 1989; 5(1):89

This chart displays the pattern of overall health financing under the current U.S. system. The 10% of the population with the lowest incomes is shown on the far left, and the highest earning 10% on the far right. The intervening bars represent the other 8 income deciles. The height of each bar indicates the proportion of income devoted to health spending for persons in that income decile (relative to the society-wide average). The poorest 10% of the population pays approximately 6 times more, as a proportion of their income, for healthcare as the wealthiest 10%.

This regressive financing pattern results from several factors. Individuals pay a large part of health costs in the U.S. Any given fixed cost (e.g., payment for a prescription, individual purchase of a policy) will represent a larger share of the income for a poor person than for a rich person. In addition, the large government subsidy for private health insurance goes mostly to the wealthy because the subsidy (like that of a tax deduction) is proportional to an individual's tax bracket. Moreover, higher income workers receive more generous insurance benefits from their employers, minimizing out-of-pocket costs.

The question of who pays for healthcare underlies much U.S. health policy debate, though it is rarely made explicit. Maintaining the current, regressive financing pattern favors the wealthy, while a tax-funded system would almost surely aid lower income individuals.

120. U.S. Corporations Wait in the Wings

We believe we can make much progress...

"We believe we can make much progress in the [WTO] negotiations to allow the opportunity for U.S. businesses to expand into foreign healthcare markets. ...public ownership of healthcare has made it difficult for U.S. private-sector healthcare providers to market in foreign countries."

—U.S. Coalition of Service Industries

U.S. firms see untapped profit opportunities in Canadian healthcare. Up to now, Canada's single payer system has largely excluded for-profit insurers, HMOs, hospitals, and other providers. In trade negotiations, U.S. industry groups and government representatives have placed a high priority on opening the service sector (including healthcare) in other nations to U.S. investment.

Protesters at the World Trade Organization (WTO) meeting in Seattle unfurled the banner shown in the photo above. It highlights the contradiction between the WTO agenda of opening every nation's markets and social service sectors (e.g., healthcare) to profit-seeking multinational firms, and the efforts of the citizens of those nations to maintain democratic control of labor, environmental, and social service conditions.

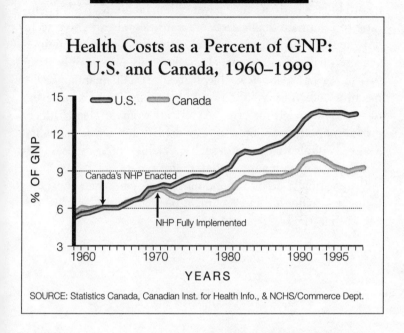

Health Costs as a Percent of GNP: U.S. and Canada, 1960–1999

SOURCE: Statistics Canada, Canadian Inst. for Health Info., & NCHS/Commerce Dept.

Many argue that we cannot afford national health insurance. Yet the national health program in Canada, as elsewhere, has effectively (perhaps too effectively) contained costs. U.S. and Canadian healthcare costs, as a percent of GNP, were almost identical until the full implementation of the Canadian national health program in 1971. Since then, Canadian costs have leveled off at about 9% of GNP, while U.S. costs have increased to about 14% of GNP. The latest data suggests that U.S. costs are again on the rise.

A single payer system facilitates cost containment in 3 ways. First, it achieves administrative savings that are unattainable under a multi-payer system. Second, the single payer is able to set and enforce overall budgetary limits. Limiting the overall health budget is difficult under our multi-payer system with hundreds of private insurers and millions of individuals paying health bills. Finally, a single payer system facilitates health planning to eliminate duplication of facilities and expensive technologies. Such duplication often wastes money and sometimes worsens quality. For instance, U.S. hospitals average only about two-thirds occupancy; we have about 10,000 mammography machines when only 5,000 would be needed to perform every test recommended for every American woman. Heart surgery provides another example of how duplication worsens quality. Many hospitals that perform such specialized procedures do too few operations to maintain their competence.

Interestingly, despite spending less on care than the U.S., Canada actually has more clinical personnel (e.g., nurses) per capita than the U.S.

123. The U.S. System is More Bureaucratized

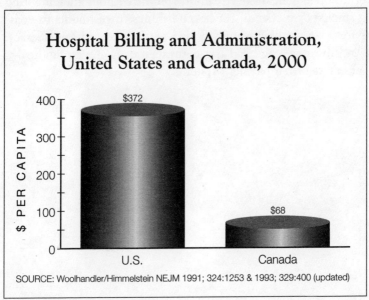

Hospital Billing and Administration, United States and Canada, 2000

SOURCE: Woolhandler/Himmelstein NEJM 1991; 324:1253 & 1993; 329:400 (updated)

Canada's single payer system has greatly simplified hospital payment, because everyone has the same insurance coverage. Canadian hospitals are paid on a global, or lump-sum budget basis rather than billing for each individual service or patient. Since hospitals send few bills to individual patients (other than Americans who get sick while visiting Canada) billing departments are tiny. The average U.S. hospital employs about 50 billing personnel; the average Canadian hospital employs 3 or 4.

In Canada, each hospital negotiates its total annual budget with the provincial health insurance program, and receives a single check each fortnight to cover virtually all costs. Hospitals need not track which patient gets each bandage or bottle of IV fluid, eliminating much of the need for detailed internal cost accounting and expensive computer billing equipment. The

U.S. could save about $80 billion each year on hospital billing by adopting a similar global budget system.

For more than a decade, entrepreneurs have touted computerization as a means to streamline billing without implementing a single payer system, yet hospitals' huge investments in computer systems have simply added to the costs of bureaucracy. And insurers' overhead has continued to rise even as they've automated their payment systems.

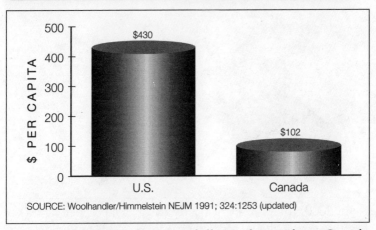

SOURCE: Woolhandler/Himmelstein NEJM 1991; 324:1253 (updated)

As with hospitals, physicians' billing is far simpler in Canada than in the U.S. Each Canadian provincial health program designs a simple billing form that is used for all patients. The physician uses the patient's insurance card to stamp the form, checks a single box, and sends all forms to the provincial insurance program by mail or computer.

All patients are covered, and bills are paid promptly. The provinces perform only minimal utilization review (i.e., review and second-guessing of doctors' treatment decisions), and do not interfere in the doctor-patient relationship. As a result, office administration and billing is far less expensive for Canadian physicians than for doctors in the United States.

The provincial government and the provincial medical association set the physicians' fee schedule through (sometimes acrimonious) negotiations. The average Canadian physician earns about 4.5 times the average Canadian industrial wage, but, as noted earlier, has far lower medical school tuition bills to pay off than their U.S. counterpart. The average U.S. physician earns about 5 times the average U.S. industrial wage.

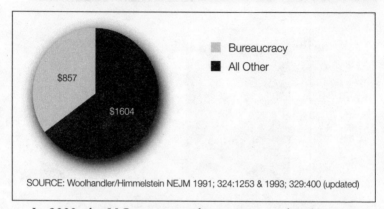

Bureaucracy
All Other

$857
$1604

SOURCE: Woolhandler/Himmelstein NEJM 1991; 324:1253 & 1993; 329:400 (updated)

In 2000, the U.S. spent nearly twice as much per capita on healthcare as Canada. More than a third of this total difference was due to excess bureaucracy in the U.S. According to studies in the New England Journal of Medicine and by the General Accounting Office (the non-partisan investigative wing of the Congress) a single payer system would save the U.S. 10% of health spending in bureaucratic costs alone, about $120 billion in savings in 2000. The savings on bureaucracy would be enough to provide coverage to all of the uninsured and improve coverage for the under-insured with no increase in health spending.

A single payer system streamlines insurance administration, as well as hospital and physician billing. Automatically enrolling everyone in a universal program eliminates insurance company advertising and sales costs. The government single payer can use the existing tax collecting agencies to garner funds with little additional administrative costs, while private insurance companies must maintain extensive premium collection bureaucracies.

Paying hospitals is also far simpler for a single payment agency than for multiple insurers. The single payer can pay hospitals a lump sum budget rather than on a per-service or per-patient basis, eliminating hundreds of millions of bills each year. Moreover, extensive insurance company efforts to shift costs onto other payers are eliminated since the single payer is responsible for virtually all bills. Health insurance overhead alone now accounts for almost 1% of Gross National Product (GNP) in the U.S., as compared to about 0.1% of GNP in Canada. U.S. private insurers keep, on average, about 14% of total premium dollars for their overhead and profits. Canada's provincial health insurance plans run for an overhead of less than 1% of total costs.

CHAPTER 11

A National Health Program and American Culture: Do They Mesh?

Americans pay a great deal for healthcare—funding princely incomes for executives and investors. Yet patients are denied care or forced to struggle to get what they need, and market values increasingly intrude into the examining room (126). Like people in other nations, Americans want a system that assures care at an affordable price, that engenders trust and respect, and affords patients choice (127). A universal, tax-funded, non-profit national health program organized like Canada's—though better funded—could achieve these goals (128).

Under such a system every American would receive a card entitling them to care at any doctor's office, hospital, clinic, etc. of their choice. (129). Hospitals, clinics, and other institutional providers would negotiate global budgets with the program, and receive a single monthly payment to cover all costs—eliminating most billing bureaucracy. Physicians in private practice would be paid based on a single negotiated fee schedule, greatly simplifying billing. For most Americans, savings from eliminating private insurance premiums would more than offset tax increases to pay for the program. The General Accounting Office, and many private-sector studies, have concluded that bureaucratic savings would offset the costs of expanding coverage to all. Some of the resources saved on bureaucracy should be devoted to upgrading long-term care, the poorest sector of our healthcare system (130). Substantial funds should also be devoted to education, income support and other transitional assistance for displaced administrative workers. Projections that national health insurance is affordable gain credibility because every other developed nation has universal coverage while spending far less than we do (131). We already have in place the facilities and human resources needed to provide care to all Americans (132).

Surveys have consistently shown wide popular support for universal coverage, though political leaders' views reflect the more conservative convictions of the business community (133). The massive donations that come largely from the wealthiest Americans sway Congress, as well as state legislators (134, 135). As a result, policy debate is dominated by options such as medical savings accounts (MSAs) and voucher programs that would undermine government oversight, raise costs, open new profit opportunities, and allow the wealthy and healthy to minimize their subsidy to working families, the sick, and the poor (136, 137). Both voucher programs and MSAs would greatly increase bureaucratic overhead, and the costs of health insurance by replacing group coverage with millions of individual policies (138).

The medical profession has, in the past, been a bulwark against national health insurance. However, many physicians have now concluded that only national health insurance can rescue our patients—and our profession. A majority of medical school faculty, students, and residents—including most medical school deans in the U.S.—support a single payer national health program (139). Once such views could be dismissed with the cold war epithet of "socialized medicine" (140). But even an iron curtain cannot forever conceal a system's failure or a solution that lies just across the border.

126. The Healthcare Americans Get

- 1/3 are uninsured or underinsured

- HMOs deny care to millions more with expensive illnesses

- Death rates higher than other wealthy nations'

- Costs double Canada's, Germany's or Sweden's—
  and rising faster

- Executives and investors making billions

- Destruction of the doctor/patient relationship

Our healthcare system is failing. It denies care to millions in need, is expensive, inefficient, and increasingly bureaucratic. The pressures of cost control, competition, and profit threaten the traditional tenets of medical practice. For patients, the fear of financial ruin amplifies the misfortune of illness. For physicians, the gratifications of healing give way to anger and alienation. Patchwork reforms succeed only in exchanging old problems for new ones. It is time to change fundamentally the trajectory of American medicine.

127. The Healthcare Americans Want

- Guaranteed access

- Free choice of doctor

- High quality

- Affordability

- Trust and respect

The U.S. currently spends enough on healthcare to provide high quality, comprehensive care to all Americans. But we cannot do so while simultaneously supporting a massive bureaucracy and diverting tens of billions of healthcare dollars to investors.

Patients want a healthcare system that is simple to navigate and responsive to their individual needs. They want care when they need it, without bureaucratic hassles; and the freedom to choose and change their caregivers, to whom they entrust their most intimate secrets, even their lives. While patients can forgive human errors, they should not tolerate the current haphazard approach to quality monitoring and improvement. Massive computer resources have been devoted to billing and utilization review, while few hospitals have computerized systems to prevent medication errors or other common, potentially lethal mistakes.

Americans want a system that assures that financial ruin will not compound the suffering of illness. The healthy and wealthy should help fund care for the sick and poor.

Finally, all Americans deserve care that respects their personal beliefs, family norms, and cultural preferences. Insurance bureaucrats should not have access to confidential medical information. The bottom-line mentality that now dominates hospitals and other health institutions must give way to a focus on human needs.

128. A National Health Program

Essentials of an NHP:

- Universal—covers everyone

- Comprehensive—all needed care, no co-pays

- Single, public payer—simplified reimbursement

- No investor-owned HMOs, hospitals, etc.

- Improved health planning

- Public accountability for equality and cost, but minimal bureaucracy

Everyone must be covered under a single comprehensive program to eliminate two-class care, assure universal access, and realize the administrative savings that are only possible under a single payer system.

All out-of-pocket payments for medically necessary services should be eliminated. Co-payments and deductibles endanger the health of the sick poor, decrease use of vital services as much as unnecessary ones, discourage preventive care, and are unwieldy and expensive to administer. Canada has few such charges, yet has lower health costs and slower cost escalation than the U.S.

A single public payer should administer health insurance in each state. This is the sine qua non of administrative simplification. Public insurance administration is far more efficient than administration by private insurers. Private insurers spend an average of 14% of premium for overhead, while Canada's public programs spend less than 1%, and the U.S. Medicare program about 2%, for overhead.

For-profit providers should be fairly compensated for existing investments and phased out. Investor-owned HMOs and health facilities provide inferior care at inflated prices.

Effective health planning requires that capital funds go to high quality, efficient programs in areas of greatest need. Today's capital spending largely determines tomorrow's operating costs, as well as the distribution of resources. Under the existing reimbursement system, which combines operating and capital payments, prosperous hospitals can expand and modernize while impoverished ones cannot, regardless of health needs or quality of services. An NHP should replace this implicit mechanism for distributing capital with an explicit one, facilitating (though not guaranteeing) allocation based on need and quality. Insulating these crucial capital allocation decisions from distortion by narrow interests will require rigorous assessment of both new technologies and community health needs, as well as active involvement of providers and patients.

Public accountability is vital, but does not require bureaucratic intrusion into the details of clinical practice. A single payer system allows the monitoring of patterns of practice, with more detailed reviews reserved for physicians with suspicious practice patterns (e.g., those who order extensive batteries of tests for every patient, or who prescribe excessive amounts of narcotics). The case-by-case oversight characteristic of current utilization review methods should be minimized, as in Canada, and in other nations with single payer systems.

129. What Would an NHP Look Like?

- Everyone receives a health care card assuring payment for all needed care

- Complete free choice of doctor & hospital

- Doctors and hospitals remain independent and non-profit, negotiate fees and budgets with NHP

- Local planning boards allocate expensive technology

- Progressive taxes go to Health Care Trust Fund

- Public agency processes and pays bills

An NHP would establish a right to comprehensive healthcare. The NHP would give each person a card guaranteeing all necessary medical care without co-payments or deductibles. The card could be used at any practitioner and at any institution. Thus, patients could freely choose their providers, and no longer face a financial threat from medical bills. Taxes would increase, but be fully offset by decreases in insurance premiums and out-of-pocket costs.

Physicians could freely choose their practice settings. Neither the patient's insurance status nor bureaucratic dictum would constrain treatment. Based on the Canadian experience, we anticipate that the NHP would cause little change in average physician income, though it might attenuate differentials between specialties. The NHP would limit the entrepreneurial aspects of medicine—the problems as well as the possibilities. Physicians could concentrate on medicine.

An NHP would sharply reduce bureaucratic interference in clinical decision-making. It would contain costs by controlling overall spending and limiting entrepreneurial incentives, obviating the need for the kind of detailed administrative oversight characteristic of HMOs. Indeed, bureaucracy intrudes less on day-to-day clinical practice in Canada (and most other countries with NHPs) than in the U.S.

130. Long-Term Care Under An NHP

- A universal right to social and medical LTC services

- Coverage for full continuum of home, community & institutional care

- Spread risk through social insurance

- Consumer choice & quality improvement

- Independent living

- Support informal caregivers

- For-profit providers phased out

SOURCE: Harrington et al. JAMA 1991; 266:3023

The long-term care system should meet the following goals:

1. Long-term care should be the right of all Americans, not a commodity available only to the wealthy and the destitute.

2. Long-term care should provide a continuum of social and medical services aimed at maximizing functional independence.

3. A progressive financing system should spread the financial risk across the entire population. The misfortune of disability should not be compounded by the specter of financial ruin. A public social insurance program is far more efficient, with lower overhead, than a private insurance program.

4. Consumers should have a range of choices and culturally appropriate options for long-term care.

5. The programs should promote high quality services and appropriate utilization in the least restrictive environment possible.

6. Medically- and socially-oriented long-term care should be coordinated with acute care.

7. The importance of informal care should be acknowledged and support, financial and other, should be offered to assist rather than supplant home and community caregivers.

8. For-profit nursing home firms, home care agencies, etc. should be replaced by community-based, non-profit organizations.

131. How Do We Know It Can Be Done?

- Every other industrialized nation has a healthcare system that assures medical care for all

- All spend less than we do; most spend less than half

- Most have lower death rates, more accountability, and higher satisfaction

We spend more than any other nation. Yet all other developed nations have achieved universal coverage. They have taken a variety of approaches. Canada's single payer system has streamlined bureaucracy while leaving patients a broad choice of providers. While the payment system in Canada is public, in many other respects the healthcare system is similar to that in the U.S. Most doctors remain in private practice and most hospitals operate as private, non-profit organizations.

The U.K.'s National Health Service owns most hospitals, and pays physicians on a salaried or modified capitation basis. This publicly-owned system is extremely efficient, though severely underfunded.

A basic truism is applicable to any system, public or private: underfunded systems have trouble providing care. Such problems are not inherent in government-funded systems—at various times national health programs have had both adequate and inadequate funding; underfunding can be corrected by increasing budgets to cover shortfalls for these very efficient systems.

The regionalized public system in Sweden, and public payment systems in Norway and Denmark, have achieved outstanding health outcomes at reasonable cost.

More pluralistic multi-payer systems, in The Netherlands and Germany, have relatively high bureaucratic costs. The multiple insurers in these systems are mostly quasi-public and highly regulated. Government sets strict ground rules for all payers and assures universal coverage.

In several of these nations, conservative governments have recently experimented with the introduction of market mechanisms in healthcare. Most have pulled back from these experiments, as bureaucratic costs and threats to equality have mounted.

132. We Have What it Takes

- Excellent hospitals, empty beds

- Enough well-trained professionals

- Superb research

- Current spending is sufficient

Fortunately, we already spend so much on healthcare in the U.S. that no additional funds are needed to assure universal, high-quality care. We have more than enough hospitals and high-technology equipment, plenty of physicians and other personnel, and an ample research budget. The challenge is to reorganize these plentiful and excellent resources to deliver the care that Americans need and deserve.

Initially, total costs under an NHP would be equivalent to health costs in the current system. Administrative savings achieved through the efficiency of a single payer system would fund improved coverage for the uninsured as well as for the tens of millions of Americans with only partial coverage. In addition, funding would be freed up to improve long-term care, retrain and assist displaced administrative workers, and for other transition costs.

Overall expenditures for hospital care would remain the same as at present. However, hospitals would be relieved of substantial administrative burdens and could transfer billing personnel and administrative resources into clinical care to meet the expected surge in demand. Similarly, physicians could save considerable time and overhead now devoted to billing hassles. Insurance overhead would be cut dramatically.

During the transition, funding that mimicked existing patterns would minimize economic disruption. All current federal funds allocated to Medicare and Medicaid would be paid to the NHP, as would all current state and local expenditures for healthcare. A tax earmarked for the NHP could be levied on all employers, with the tax rate set so that total collections equaled the previous year's total of employers' expenditures for health benefits, adjusted for inflation. Additional taxes equivalent to the amount now spent by individuals for insurance premiums and out-of-pocket costs could be levied.

It is critical that all funds for healthcare flow through the NHP. Such single-source payment has been the cornerstone of cost containment and administrative efficiency in Canada. Overall, the average American would pay no more for healthcare under the NHP than they do at present. However, rather than paying insurance premiums, co-payments, deductibles, property taxes used to fund health benefits for municipal employees, etc., we would pay earmarked healthcare taxes.

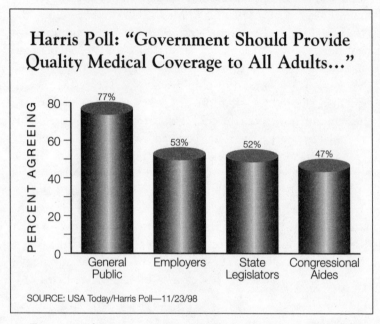

Harris Poll: "Government Should Provide Quality Medical Coverage to All Adults..."

PERCENT AGREEING

General Public	77%
Employers	53%
State Legislators	52%
Congressional Aides	47%

SOURCE: USA Today/Harris Poll—11/23/98

For more than twenty years, polls have shown wide public support for government-assured universal healthcare coverage. But those closest to the seat of power are least likely to concur with the public.

Some health policy experts argue that "cultural differences" make Americans scornful of a Canadian-style system. But, Americans and Canadians have similar views on healthcare. More than 80% of persons polled in each nation favor "one-class care"; more than three-quarters believe that government should assure access to care; and about two-thirds advocate taxing the rich to pay for care. Fewer than one in five believe the sick should pay more for care.

134. Democracy for Sale

The Billion $ Congress

Contribution Type	Amount
Direct to Candidates	$781.3 million
Hard Money to National Party	$445 million
Soft Money to National Party	$224.4 million
Issue Advertising	$112 million (est)
Independent Expenditures	$11.7 million
Total	**$1,574.4 million**

SOURCE: www.publicampaign.org

Our healthcare system is the bitter fruit of our rotten campaign finance system. The exigencies of fundraising dominate our Congressional and Presidential campaigns. Candidates are beholden to wealthy donors.

Drug firms alone spent $83.6 million on lobbying in 1999, employing 297 lobbyists—about one for every two members of Congress. Senator Orrin Hatch received $169,000 from drug firms in a single year, including $14,000 from Schering-Plough. Coincidentally, Hatch drafted a bill that would extend the patent life on Schering's allergy drug, Claritin. Two other Senators favoring patent extension—Republican John Ashcroft and Democrat Robert Torricelli—have recently received $50,000 donations from Schering.

However, we retain the democratic right to oust our politicians and reform our nation. America's history is replete with examples of powerful social movements kindled by initially unimposing moral voices: in the 18th century the Boston Tea Party; in the 19th, abolitionism; and in the 20th century, appeals for civil rights and nuclear disarmament. Only a comparable public outcry can reclaim our politics and our healthcare.

135. Wealth Buys Political Power

- The 107,000 residents of zip code 10021 gave $1.5 million to 1999 presidential campaigns, and $9.3 million to 1996 congressional races

- The residents of New Hampshire gave $333,000 to presidential candidates in 1999

- The 9.5 million people in communities that are >90% minority gave $5.5 million in 1996 Congressional races

- In 1996, 91% of Congressional races were won by the candidate who spent the most

- Since 1984, the candidate with the most money on January 1 of the election year always wins his party's nomination

SOURCE: www.publicampaign.org

National health insurance threatens the profits of insurers, HMOs, hospital and drug firms, and a panoply of other powerful private interests whose voices are amplified by money. In the absence of a powerful grassroots mobilization, a handful of wealthy individuals and corporations have free rein to shape health policy.

136. Medical Savings Accounts: No Savings

- Sickest 10% of Americans use 72% of care. MSAs cannot lower these catastrophic costs

- The 15% of people who get no care would get premium "refunds," removing their cross-subsidy for the sick, but not lowering use or cost

- Discourages prevention

- Complex to administer—insurers have to keep track of all out-of-pocket payments

- Congressional Budget Office projects that MSAs would increase Medicare costs by $2 billion

Medical savings accounts (MSAs) combine high deductible (e.g., $5,000) insurance policies with tax subsidies for savings accounts that can be used to pay the deductibles. The individual can, at a later date, withdraw any money not spent on medical services.

MSAs have several problems. First, a small number of very sick people account for most medical expenditures. Since these very sick patients rapidly exceed the deductible threshold, the incentives in MSA plans could not lower the almost three-fourths of total U.S. medical care costs that they incur.

Second, MSAs selectively reduce preventive care. Patients have discretion over preventive care like pap smears or blood pressure checks, and presumably would choose to receive less if they had MSAs. Conversely, care for the consequences of failed prevention (e.g., cervical cancer or stroke) is much more urgent, and hence less likely to be reduced by the financial incentives of MSAs.

Third, studies show that steep co-payments cut care for serious as well as trivial symptoms.

Fourth, MSAs remove cross subsidies from the healthy to the sick. The idea of health insurance is that everyone, healthy or sick, pays into the insurance pool, but only the sick draw out of it. With MSAs the roughly 15% of people who need no medical care in the course of a year would get premium refunds. This would not lower healthcare costs (these people were receiving no care anyway) but would leave a shortfall in the funds available to cover the sick.

Fifth, MSA's are complex and expensive to administer. Insurers and individuals must keep detailed records of all out-of-pocket payments to document when someone exceeds the deductible. Hence, MSAs don't reduce insurance overhead. In addition banks or other institutions have to administer the actual accounts adding to bureaucratic costs.

137. What's Wrong with Tax Subsidies and Vouchers?

- Taxes go to wasteful private insurers, overhead > 13%

- Amounts too low for good coverage, especially for the sick

- High costs for little coverage—much of subsidy replaces employer-paid coverage

- Encourages shift from employer-based to individual policies with overhead of 35% or more

- Costs continue to rise (e.g. FEHBP)

- Many are unable to purchase wisely— e.g. frail elders, severely ill, poor literacy

Vouchers and tax subsidies feature heavily in both Republican and Democratic proposals to expand coverage and reform Medicare. Such programs would offer recipients a government voucher or subsidy to purchase private coverage.

Medicare voucher or "premiums support" proposals would abolish Medicare's guarantee to pay for covered services. Instead, Medicare would give seniors a voucher, which they could supplement with their own money, to purchase private insurance. The voucher would cover a bare-bones plan—at least initially. Over time, the value of the voucher would likely increase more slowly than health costs, leaving seniors to pick up an increasing share of costs. Obviously, the wealthy could afford better coverage.

All voucher proposals funnel tax dollars for care through wasteful private insurers. In a $100 billion voucher program, private insurers would skim off about $15 billion for overhead and profits; only $85 billion would be available for care. The same $100 billion spent through traditional Medicare would buy $98 billion worth of care.

Moreover, actual experience contradicts the market theory behind vouchers. Economists predicted that voucher programs would help contain costs as patients shopped around for the best insurance deal. But costs in model programs (like the Federal Employees Health Benefits Program) have risen faster than Medicare costs.

Finally, in demonstration projects, subsidies for low income workers to purchase private insurance have failed. Generally the subsidies are too small to entice many of the low income uninsured to buy coverage, and many of those who do draw the new subsidies were already covered. In effect, tax dollars replace private dollars but few of the uninsured get coverage.

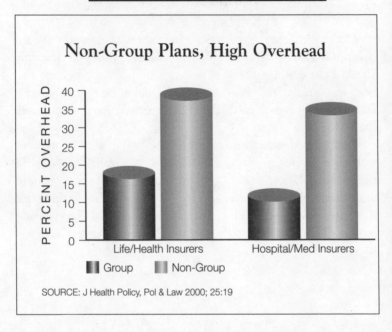

Non-Group Plans, High Overhead

SOURCE: J Health Policy, Pol & Law 2000; 25:19

The American Medical Association (which now counts only 40% of doctors as members) and several conservative groups have recommended replacing employment-based coverage, or Medicare, with individually-purchased plans.

Unfortunately, such individually-purchased ("non-group") plans have huge overhead costs—more than 30% of total premiums. Hence, shifting Americans from current employment-based group coverage to individual non-group plans would more than double our already bloated insurance administration costs.

139. Fifty-seven Percent of Medical Students & Faculty Favor Single Payer

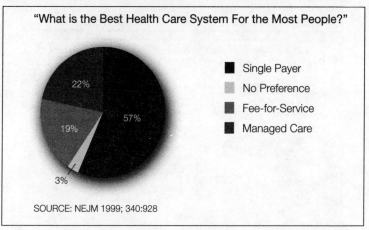

"What is the Best Health Care System For the Most People?"

- Single Payer
- No Preference
- Fee-for-Service
- Managed Care

57%
22%
19%
3%

SOURCE: NEJM 1999; 340:928

In several polls over the past 30 years, about two-thirds of Americans have supported national health insurance. But wide physician support for such reform is new. In a nationwide poll of medical students, interns, residents, medical school faculty, and deans published in 1999, 57% favored single payer national health insurance as the best option. Indeed, a majority of each of these groups—including most deans—endorsed national health insurance.

140. A Communist Plot?

CHAPTER 12

A National Health Program for the United States

A PHYSICIANS' PROPOSAL

DAVID U. HIMMELSTEIN, M.D.,
STEFFIE WOOLHANDLER, M.D., M.P.H., AND
THE WRITING COMMITTEE OF THE WORKING GROUP
ON PROGRAM DESIGN*

Our healthcare system is failing. It denies access to many in need and is expensive, inefficient, and increasingly bureaucratic. The pressures of cost control, competition, and profit threaten the traditional tenets of medical practice. For patients, the misfortune of illness is often amplified by the fear of financial ruin. For physicians, the gratifications of healing often give way to anger and alienation. Patchwork reforms succeed only in exchanging old problems for new ones. It is time to change fundamentally the trajectory of American medicine—to develop a comprehensive national health program for the United States.

We are physicians active in the full range of medical endeavors. We are primary care doctors and surgeons, psychiatrists and public health specialists, pathologists and administrators. We work in hospitals, clinics, private practices, health maintenance organizations (HMOs), universities, corporations, and public

*This proposal was drafted by a 30 member Writing Committee, then reviewed and endorsed by 412 other physicians representing virtually every state and medical specialty. A full list of endorsers is available on request.

agencies. Some of us are young, still in training; others are greatly experienced, and some have held senior positions in American medicine.

As physicians, we constantly confront the irrationality of the present healthcare system. In private practice, we waste countless hours on billing and bureaucracy. For uninsured patients, we avoid procedures, consultations, and costly medications. Diagnosis-related groups (DRGs) have placed us between administrators demanding early discharge and elderly patients with no one to help at home—all the while glancing over our shoulders at the peer-review organization. In HMOs we walk a tightrope between thrift and penuriousness, too often under the pressure of surveillance by bureaucrats more concerned with the bottom line than with other measures of achievement. In public health work we are frustrated in the face of plenty; the world's richest healthcare system is unable to insure such basic services as prenatal care and immunizations.

Despite our disparate perspectives, we are united by dismay at the current state of medicine and by the conviction that an alternative must be developed. We hope to spark debate, to transform disaffection with what exists into a vision of what might be. To this end, we submit for public review, comment, and revision a working plan for a rational and humane healthcare system—a national health program.

We envisage a program that would be federally mandated and ultimately funded by the federal government but administered largely at the state and local level. The proposed system would eliminate financial barriers to care, minimize economic incentives for both excessive and insufficient care, discourage administrative interference and expense, improve the distribution of health facilities, and control costs by curtailing bureaucracy and fostering health planning. Our plan borrows many features from the Canadian national health program and adapts them to the unique circumstances of the United States. We suggest that, as in Canada's provinces, the national health program be tested initially in statewide demonstration projects. Thus, our proposal addresses both the structure of the national health program and the transition process necessary to implement the program in a single state. In each section below, we present a key feature of the proposal, followed by the rationale for our approach. Areas such as long-term care; public, occupational, environmental, and mental health; and medical education need much more development and will be addressed in detail in future proposals.

Coverage

Everyone would be included in a single public plan covering all medically necessary services, including acute, rehabilitative, long-term, and home care; mental health services; dental services; occupational healthcare; prescription drugs and medical supplies; and preventive and public health measures. Boards of experts and community representatives would determine which services were unnecessary or ineffective, and these would be excluded from coverage. As in Canada, alternative insurance coverage for services covered under the national health program would be eliminated, as would patient co-payments and deductibles.

Universal coverage would solve the gravest problem in healthcare by eliminating financial barriers to care. A single comprehensive program is necessary both to ensure equal access to care and to minimize the complexity and expense of billing and administration. The public administration of insurance funds would save tens of billions of dollars each year. The more than 1500 private insurers in the United States now consume about 8 percent of revenues for overhead, whereas both the Medicare program and the Canadian national health program have overhead costs of only 2 to 3 percent. The complexity of our current insurance system, with its multiplicity of payers, forces U.S. hospitals to spend more than twice as much as Canadian hospitals on billing and administration and requires U.S. physicians to spend about 10 percent of their gross incomes on excess billing costs. Eliminating insurance programs that duplicated the national health program coverage, though politically thorny, would clearly be within the prerogative of Congress. Failure to do so would also require the continuation of the costly bureaucracy necessary to administer and deal with such programs.

Copayments and deductibles endanger the health of poor people who are sick, decrease the use of vital inpatient medical services as much as they discourage the use of unnecessary ones, discourage preventive care, and are unwieldy and expensive to administer. Canada has few such charges, yet health costs are lower than in the United States and have risen slowly. In the United States, in contrast, increasing co-payments and deductibles have failed to slow the escalation of costs.

Instead of the confused and often unjust dictates of insurance companies, a greatly expanded program of technology assessment and cost-effectiveness evaluation would guide decisions about covered services, as well as about the allocation of funds for capital spending, drug formularies, and other issues.

Payment for Hospital Services

Each hospital would receive a lump-sum payment to cover all operating expenses—a "global" budget. The amount of this payment would be negotiated with the state national health program payment board and would be based on past expenditures, previous financial and clinical performance, projected changes in levels of services, wages and other costs, and proposed new and innovative programs. Hospitals would not bill for services covered by the national health program. No part of the operating budget could be used for hospital expansion, profit, marketing, or major capital purchases or leases. These expenditures would also come from the national health program fund, but monies for them would be appropriated separately.

Global prospective budgeting would simplify hospital administration and virtually eliminate billing, thus freeing up substantial resources for increased clinical care. Before the nationwide implementation of the national program, hospitals in the states with demonstration programs could bill out-of-state patients on a simple per diem basis. Prohibiting the use of operating funds for capital purchases or profit would eliminate the main financial incentive for both excessive intervention (under fee-for-service payment) and skimping on care (under DRG-type prospective payment systems), since neither inflating revenues nor limiting care would result in gain for the institution. The separate appropriation of funds explicitly designated for capital expenditures would facilitate rational health planning. In Canada, this method of hospital payment has been successful in containing costs, minimizing bureaucracy, improving the distribution of health resources, and maintaining the quality of care. It shifts the focus of hospital administration away from the bottom line and toward the provision of optimal clinical services.

Payment for Physician Services, Ambulatory Care, and Medical Home Care

To minimize the disruption of existing patterns of care, the national health program would include three payment options for physicians and other practitioners: fee-for-service payment, salaried positions in institutions receiving global budgets, and salaried positions within group practices or HMOs receiving per capita (capitation) payments.

Fee-for-Service Payment

The state national health program payment board and a representative of the fee-for-service practitioners (perhaps the state medical society) would negotiate a simplified, binding fee schedule. Physicians would submit bills to the national health program on a simple form or by computer and would receive extra payment for any bill not paid within 30 days. Payments to physicians would cover only the service provided by physicians and their support staff and would exclude reimbursement for costly capital purchases of equipment for the office, such as CT scanners. Physicians who accepted payment from the national health program could bill patients directly only for uncovered services (as is done for cosmetic surgery in Canada).

Global Budgets

Institutions such as hospitals, health centers, group practices, clinics serving migrant workers, and medical home care agencies could elect to receive a global budget for the delivery of outpatient care, home care, and physicians' services, as well as for preventive healthcare and patient-education programs. The negotiation process and the regulations covering capital expenditures and profits would be similar to those for inpatient hospital services. Physicians employed in such institutions would be salaried.

Capitation

HMOs, group practices, and other institutions could elect to be paid fees on a per capita basis to cover all outpatient care, physicians' services, and medical home care. The regulations covering the use of such payments for capital expenditures and for profits would be similar to those that would apply to hospitals. The capitation fee would not cover inpatient services (except care provided by a physician), which would be included in hospitals' global budgets. Selective enrollment policies would be prohibited, and patients would be permitted to leave an HMO or other health plan with appropriate notice. Physicians working in HMOs would be salaried, and financial incentives to physicians based on the HMO's financial performance would be prohibited.

The diversity of existing practice arrangements, each with strong proponents, necessitates a pluralistic approach. Under all three proposed options, capital purchase and profits would be uncoupled from payments to physicians and other operating costs—a feature that is essential for minimizing entrepreneurial incentives, containing costs, and facilitating health planning.

Under the fee-for-service option, physicians' office overhead would be reduced by the simplification of billing. The improved coverage would encourage preventive care. In Canada, fee-for-service practice with negotiated fee schedules and mandatory assignment (acceptance of the assigned fee as total payment) has proved to be compatible with cost containment, adequate incomes for physicians, and a high level of access to and satisfaction with care on the part of patients. The Canadian provinces have responded to the inflationary potential of fee-for-service payment in various ways: by limiting the number of physicians, by monitoring physicians for outlandish practice patterns, by setting overall limits on a province's spending for physicians' services (thus relying on the profession to police itself), and even by capping the total reimbursement of individual physicians. These regulatory options have been made possible (and have not required an extensive bureaucracy) because all payment comes from a single source. Similar measures might be needed in the United States, although our penchant for bureaucratic hypertrophy might require a concomitant cap on spending for the regulatory apparatus. For example, spending for program administration and reimbursement bureaucracy might be restricted to 3 percent of total costs.

Global budgets for institutional providers would eliminate billing, while providing a predictable and stable source of income. Such funding could also encourage the development of preventive health programs in the community, such as education programs on the acquired immunodeficiency syndrome

(AIDS), whose costs are difficult to attribute and bill to individual patients.

Continuity of care would no longer be disrupted when patients' insurance coverage changed as a result of retirement or job change. Incentives for providers receiving capitation payments to skimp on care would be minimized, since unused operating funds could not be devoted to expansion or profit.

Payment for Long-Term Care

A separate proposal for long-term care is under development, guided by three principles. First, access to care should be based on need rather than on age or ability to pay. Second, social and community-based services should be expanded and integrated with institutional care. Third, bureaucracy and entrepreneurial incentives should be minimized through global budgeting with separate funding for capital expenses.

[Editors note: This proposal appeared in the *Journal of the American Medical Association*; Volume 266, pages 3023–3029.]

Allocation of Capital Funds, Health Planning, and Return on Equity

Funds for the construction or renovation of health facilities and for purchases of major equipment would be appropriated from the national health program budget. The funds would be distributed by state and regional health planning boards composed of both experts and community representatives. Capital projects funded by private donations would require approval by the health planning board if they entailed an increase in future operating expenses.

The national health program would pay owners of for-profit hospitals, nursing homes, and clinics a reasonable fixed rate of return on existing equity. Since virtually all new capital investment would be funded by the national health program, it would not be included in calculating the return on equity.

Current capital spending greatly affects future operating cost, as well as the distribution of resources. Effective health planning requires that funds go to high-quality, efficient programs in the areas of greatest need. Under the existing reimbursement system, which combines operating and capital payments, prosperous hospitals can expand and modernize, whereas impoverished ones cannot, regardless of the health needs of the population they serve or the quality of service they provide. The national health program would replace this implicit mechanism for distributing capital with an explicit one, which would facilitate (though not guarantee) allocation on the basis of need and equality. Insulating these crucial decisions from distortion by narrow interests would require the rigorous evaluation of new technology and assessment of needs, as well as the active involvement of providers and patients.

For-profit providers would be compensated for existing investments. Since new for-profit investment would be barred, the proprietary sector would gradually shrink.

Public, Environmental, and Occupational Health Services

Existing arrangements for public, occupational, and environmental health services would be retained in the short term. Funding for preventive healthcare would be expanded. Additional proposals dealing with these issues are planned.

Prescription Drugs and Supplies

An expert panel would establish and regularly update a list of all necessary and useful drugs and outpatient equipment. Suppliers would bill the national health program directly for the wholesale cost, plus a reasonable dispensing fee, of any item on the list that was prescribed by a licensed practitioner. The substitution of generic for proprietary drugs would be encouraged.

Funding

The national health program would disburse virtually all payments for health service. The total expenditure would be set at the same proportion of the GNP as health costs represented in the year preceding the establishment of the national health program. Funds for the national health program could be raised through a variety of mechanisms. In the long run, funding based on an income tax or other progressive tax might be the fairest and most efficient solution, since tax-based funding is the least cumbersome and least expensive mechanism for collecting money. During the transition period in states with demonstration programs, the following structure would mimic existing funding patterns and minimize economic disruption.

Medicare and Medicaid

All current and federal funds allocated to Medicare and Medicaid would be paid to the national health program. The contribution of each program would be based on the previous year's expenditures, adjusted for inflation. Using Medicare and Medicaid funds in this manner would require a federal waiver.

State and Local Funds

All current state and local funds for healthcare expenditures, adjusted for inflation, would be paid to the national health program.

Employer Contributions

A tax earmarked for the national health program would be levied on all employers. The tax rate would be set so that total collections equaled the previous year's statewide total of employers' expenditures for health benefits, adjusted for inflation. Employers obligated by preexisting contracts to provide health benefits could credit the cost of those benefits toward their national health program tax liability.

Private Insurance Revenues

Private health insurance plans duplicating the coverage of the national health program would be phased out over three years. During this transition period, all revenues from such plans would be turned over to the national health program, after the deduction of a reasonable fee to cover the costs of collecting premiums.

General Tax Revenues

Additional taxes, equivalent to the amount now spent by individual citizens for insurance premiums and out-of-pocket health costs, would be levied.

It would be critical for all funds for healthcare to flow through the national health program. Such single-source payment (monopsony) has been the cornerstone of cost containment and health planning in Canada. The mechanism of raising funds for the national health program would be a matter of tax policy, largely separate from the organization of the healthcare system itself. As in Canada, federal funding could attenuate inequalities among the states in financial and medical resources.

The transitional proposal for demonstration programs in selected states illustrates how monopsony payment could be established with limited disruption of existing patterns of healthcare funding. The employers' contribution would represent a decrease in costs for most firms that now provide health insurance and an increase for those that do not currently pay for benefits. Some provision might be needed to cushion the impact of the change on financially strapped small businesses. Decreased individual spending for healthcare would offset the additional tax burden on individual citizens. Private health insurance, with its attendant inefficiency and waste, would be largely eliminated. A program of job replacement and retraining for insurance and hospital-billing employees would be an important component of the program during the transition period.

Discussion

The Patient's View

The national health program would establish a right to comprehensive healthcare. As in Canada, each person would receive a national health program card entitling him or her to all necessary medical care without co-payments or deductibles. The card could be used with any fee-for-service practitioner and at any institution receiving a global budget. HMO members could receive nonemergency care only through their HMO, although they could readily transfer to the non-HMO option.

Thus, patients would have a free choice of providers, and the financial threat of illness would be eliminated. Taxes would increase by an amount equivalent to the current total of medical expenditures by individuals. Conversely, individuals' aggregate payments for medical care would decrease by the same amount.

The Practitioner's View

Physicians would have a free choice of practice settings. Treatment would no longer be constrained by the patient's insurance status or by bureaucratic dicta. On the basis of the Canadian experience, we anticipate that the average physician's income would change little, although differences among specialties might be attenuated.

Fee-for-service practitioners would be paid for the care of anyone not enrolled in an HMO. The entrepreneurial aspects of medicine—with the attendant problems as well as possibilities—would be limited. Physicians could concentrate on medicine; every patient would be fully insured, but physicians could increase their income only by providing more care. Billing would involve imprinting the patient's national health program card on a charge slip, checking a box to indicate the complexity of the procedure or service, and sending the slip (or computer record) to the physician-payment board. This simplification of billing would save thousands of dollars per practitioner in annual office expenses.

Bureaucratic interference in clinical decision-making would sharply diminish. Costs would be contained by controlling overall spending and by limiting entrepreneurial incentives, thus obviating the need for the kind of detailed administrative oversight that is characteristic of the DRG program and similar schemes. Indeed, there is much less administrative intrusion in day-to-day clinical practice in Canada (and most other countries with national health programs) than in the United States.

Salaried practitioners would be insulated from the financial consequences of clinical decisions. Because savings on patient care could no longer be used for institutional expansion or profits, the pressure to skimp on care would be minimized.

The Effect on Other Health Workers

Nurses and other healthcare personnel would enjoy a more humane and efficient clinical milieu. The burdens of paperwork associated with billing would be lightened. The jobs of many administrative and insurance employees would be eliminated, necessitating a major effort at job placement and retraining. We advocate that many of these displaced workers be deployed in expanded programs of public health, health promotion and education, and home care and as support personnel to free-up nurses for clinical tasks.

The Effect on Hospitals

Hospitals' revenues would become stable and predictable. More than half the current hospital bureaucracy would be eliminated, and the remaining administrators could focus on facilitating clinical care and planning for future health needs.

The capital budget requests of hospitals would be weighed against other priorities for healthcare investment. Hospitals would neither grow because they were profitable nor fail because of unpaid bills—although regional health planning would undoubtedly mandate that some expand and others close or be put to other uses. Responsiveness to community needs, the quality of care, efficiency, and innovation would replace financial performance as the bottom line. The elimination of new for-profit investment would lead to a gradual conversion of proprietary hospitals to not-for-profit status.

The Effect on the Insurance Industry

The insurance industry would feel the greatest impact of this proposal. Private insurance firms would have no role in health-care financing, since the public administration of insurance is more efficient, and single-source payment is the key to both equal access and cost control. Indeed, most of the extra funds needed to finance the expansion of care would come from eliminating the overhead and profits of insurance companies and abolishing the billing apparatus necessary to apportion costs among the various plans.

The Effect on Corporate America

Firms that now provide generous employee health benefits would realize savings, because their contribution to the national health program would be less than their current health insurance costs. Since most firms that compete in international markets would save money, the competitiveness of U.S. products would be enhanced. However, costs would increase for employers that do not now provide health benefits. The average healthcare costs for employers would be unchanged in the short run. In the long run, overall health costs would rise less steeply because of improved health planning and greater efficiency. The funding mechanism ultimately adopted would determine the corporate share of those costs.

Health Benefits and Financial Costs

There is ample evidence that removing financial barriers to healthcare encourages timely care and improves health. After Canada instituted a national health program, visits to physicians increased among patients with serious symptoms. Mortality rates, which were higher than U.S. rates through the

1950s and early 1960s, fell below those in the United States. In the Rand Health Insurance Experiment, free care reduced the annual risk of dying by 10% among the 25% of U.S. adults at highest risk. Conversely, cuts in California's Medicaid program led to worsening health. Strong circumstantial evidence links the poor U.S. record on infant mortality with inadequate access to prenatal care.

We expect that the national health program would cause little change in the total costs of ambulatory and hospital care; savings on administration and billing (about 10% of current healthcare spending) would approximately offset the costs of expanded services. Indeed, current low hospital-occupancy rates suggest that the additional care could be provided at low cost. Similarly, many physicians with empty appointment slots could take on more patients without added office, secretarial, or other overhead costs. However, the expansion of long-term care (under any system) would increase costs. The experience in Canada suggests that the increased demand for acute care would be modest after an initial surge, and that improvements in health planning and cost containment made possible by single source payment would slow the escalation of healthcare costs. Vigilance would be needed to stem the regrowth of costly and intrusive bureaucracy.

Unsolved Problems

Our brief proposal leaves many vexing problems unsolved. Much detailed planning would be needed to ease dislocations during the implementation of the program. Neither the encouragement of preventive healthcare and healthful lifestyles nor improvements in occupational and environmental health would automatically follow from the institution of a national health program. Similarly, racial, linguistic, geographic, and other nonfinancial barriers to access would persist. The need for quality assurance and continuing medical education would be no less pressing. High medical school tuitions that skew specialty choices and discourage low-income applicants, the under-representation of minorities, the role of foreign medical graduates, and other issues in medical education would remain. Some patients would still seek inappropriate emergency care, and some physicians might still succumb to the temptation to increase their incomes by encouraging unneeded services. The malpractice crisis would be only partially ameliorated. The 25% of judgments now awarded for future medical costs would be eliminated but our society would remain litigious, and legal and insurance fees would still consume about two-thirds of all malpractice premiums. Establishing research priorities and directing funds to high-quality investigations would be no easier. Much further work in the area of long-term care would be required. Regional health planning and capital allocation would make possible, but not ensure, the fair and efficient allocation of resources. Finally, although insurance coverage for patients with AIDS would be ensured, the need for expanded prevention and research and for new models of care would continue. Although all these problems would not be solved, a national health program would establish a framework for addressing them.

Political Prospects

Our proposal would undoubtedly encounter powerful opponents in the health insurance industry, firms that do not provide health benefits to employees, and medical entrepreneurs. However, we also have allies. Most physicians (56%) support some form of national health program, although 74% are convinced that most other doctors oppose it. Many of the largest corporations would enjoy substantial savings if our proposal were adopted. Most significantly, the great majority of Americans support a universal, comprehensive, publicly administered national health program, as shown by virtually every opinion poll in the past 30 years. If mobilized, such public conviction could override even the most strenuous private opposition.

PNHP

Physicians for a National Health Program is a nationwide group of 9,000 physicians with chapters in more than 35 states. PNHP advocates for publicly funded, non-profit national health insurance.

Physicians for a National Health Program
332 S. Michigan, Suite 500
Chicago, IL 60604

www.pnhp.org

Other information on single payer health plans is available
at www.allies-now.com

About the Authors

David U. Himmelstein and Steffie Woolhandler are founders of Physicians for a National Health Program. They teach and practice medicine at Harvard Medical School and the Cambridge Hospital.

Dr. Ida Hellander is the Executive Director of the Chicago-based Physicians for a National Health Program. She received her M.D. from the University of Minnesota Medical School in 1989 and her B.A. in Economics from Yale in 1984. Her research interests include the corporatization of healthcare and international health systems, particularly the Scandinavian health systems.